MEDIA AND
DEVELOPMENT

DEVELOPMENT **MATTERS**

MARTIN SCOTT

Zed Books

LONDON | NEW YORK

Media and Development was first published in 2014 by Zed Books Ltd, 7 Cynthia Street, London N1 9JF, UK and Room 400, 175 Fifth Avenue, New York, NY 10010, USA

www.zedbooks.co.uk

Copyright © Martin Scott 2014

Index: ed.emery@thefreeuniversity.net
Cover designed by www.kikamiller.com
Printed and bound by CPI Group (UK) Ltd, Croydon, CR0 4YY

Distributed in the USA exclusively by Palgrave Macmillan, a division of St Martin's Press, LLC, 175 Fifth Avenue, New York, NY 10010, USA

A catalogue record for this book is available from the British Library
Library of Congress Cataloging in Publication Data available

ISBN   978-1-78032-551-4 hb
ISBN   978-1-78032-550-7 pb

MIX
Paper from responsible sources
FSC   FSC® C013604
www.fsc.org

DEVELOPMENT **MATTERS**

About the series

The Development Matters series is made up of comprehensive texts to key development issues. It draws on Zed's progressive political tradition by offering politically engaged and challenging critiques and a commitment to the voices of the poor. The series demonstrates academic and conceptual rigour to provide readers with a critical, reflexive and challenging exploration of the pressing concerns in development. It also includes cross-cutting themes that challenge traditional disciplinary, ideological and theory–practice boundaries.

About the author

Dr Martin Scott is a lecturer in media and international develop-ment at the University of East Anglia. His research is primarily concerned with media coverage of development and the global South. He has also written about entertainment education, media literacy and the role of popular culture in engaging young people in politics.

Contents

Figures and tables

Figures

Tables

Acknowledgements

My thanks to Helen Yanacopulos, who encouraged me to write this book, and to Kim Walker, who has enabled me to publish it. I am also grateful to the many colleagues who have read and commented on early drafts of this work, including Akim Mogaji, Amanda Barnes, Dan Brockington, David Girling, Heather Savigny, Isla McIntosh, John Street, Karen Merkel, Kate Lloyd Morgan, Kayonaaz Kalyanwala, Mark Galloway, Rachael Borlase, Rosie Smith, Sally-Ann Wilson, Shani Orgad, Sophie Chalk, Thomas Tufte and Viviane Lucia Fluck. The faults in this text remain my own. I am especially grateful to the many students on the MA course in Media and International Development from whom I have learnt so much, including Amy Richardson, Ana Libisch, Andria Solomonidou, Arshia Aziz, Barclay Martin, Isaac Barnes, Beth Titchiner, Chantal Foyer, Chenchen Zhu, Colleen Braganza, Connor Botkin, Daisy Serem, Daniel Presecan, Elisa Blin, Fiona Dolan, Gina Adams, Guipeng Wu, Isabella De Grave, Jason Sayler, Jeremy Dales, Jiahui Li, Jiangyu Zhou, Jing Chen, Juexi Qian, Julia Loosen, Kayo Kalyanwala, Kristian Porter, Kyoko Takahashi, Leah Braverman, Lijiaxiu Zhang, Masayu Vinanda, Nami Higashikawa, Nanako Sugimura, Naomi Herron, Natalia Reyes Hernandez, Niki Taigel, Panita Mahanonda, Pascal Ryffel, Rosemary Gaisie, Rosie Smith, Sam Howard, Sandra Milena Rodriguez-Rojas, Si-juan Wang, Simran Singh, Suzanne Harris, Tao Wu, Thomas Reid, Tripura Oli, Wansawang Temchamnarn, Wiriya Kingwatcharapong, Xiuwen Zhu, Yile Zhou, Yuan Gao, Yutong Zhang, Zhai Zhai, Zilani Khonje.

Introduction

What role can media play in addressing (or exacerbating) poverty and inequality? As the processes of mediatization and globalization increasingly transform the ways in which we live our lives (see Hemer and Tufte 2012), this is a key question of our time and it is the central question of this book.

It is not difficult to find examples that illustrate the role of media in international development. While the mobilizing power of social media in the Arab Spring is perhaps the most obvious example, the list of other phenomena is long and growing. Images of starving children used for fund-raising, soap operas designed to prompt social change, the training of journalists in fragile states, campaigns for freedom of information laws, foreign news coverage of humanitarian crises and participatory video projects are just some of the many manifestations of the relationship between media and development. Media not only increase our access to knowledge of events happening around the world, but also (seemingly) enable us to influence them. Development organizations across the globe are themselves increasingly being 'mediatized', or shaped by a media logic (Jones forthcoming). More broadly, media are ever more involved in international relations and what has been described as the recent 'fourth wave' of democratic political transformations (Howard and Hussain 2013).

Such examples and grand claims are characteristic of much of the discourse in this area and are useful for helping to draw attention to the importance of media in development.

Unfortunately, though, they teach us very little about the complexities and contingencies of the relationship between international development and media. While it may be useful in some contexts to draw attention to the potential benefits of media, the danger is that this comes at the expense of developing a more critical appreciation of the contexts in which media-related interventions can work, when they are not appropriate and the conditions upon which their effectiveness depends. Anecdotes and aggrandizing are not sound bases for project design or policy-making.

To acquire a more informed perspective on the role of the media, we need to develop a critical understanding of a wide range of relevant theories, practices and approaches which link different aspects of development to different dimensions of the media. This book provides such an understanding by offering concise and original critical introductions to the three fields of communication for development (C4D), media development and media representations of development. In doing so, it also begins to identify some of the lessons we can learn from a closer integration of these three fields.

Three ways of thinking about media and development

Communication for development (C4D) In 2006, the Rome Consensus from the World Congress on Communication for Development (C4D) defined C4D as 'a social process based on dialogue using a broad range of tools and methods. It is also about seeking change at different levels, including listening, building trust, sharing knowledge and skills, building policies, debating and learning for sustained and meaningful change. It is not public relations or corporate communication.'

Chapters 1 and 2 of this book are devoted to providing a critical introduction to the two approaches that define this broad field. Chapter 1 sets out the key defining features of a media for development (M4D) approach in which media are seen as instruments for changing individuals' norms and behaviours. It also equips readers with a critical perspective on this approach and an understanding of the various hybrid forms which it can adopt. To achieve this, the work of specific examples is reviewed throughout, including Development Media International, the Population Media Centre, Soul City and *Makutano Junction*. Chapter 2 seeks to illustrate the different, complex and often contradictory forms that a participatory approach to using media in development can take. By posing multiple questions for the reader to consider, rather than offering clear answers, the format of the chapter itself actively highlights a participatory approach to communication.

There is a strong sense within the C4D community that this field is unfairly neglected in international development and that this severely hinders the effectiveness of development interventions. In *At the Heart of Change*, Mark Wilson and Kitty Warnock (2007: 7) argue that one of the main reasons for the 'slow progress' towards the Millennium Development Goals (MDGs) was the 'failure to recognise that open, inclusive, participatory communication and information processes are prerequisites for successful, sustainable development'. It is in this context that Alfonso Gumucio-Dagron (2008: 655) described communication as 'until very recently the fifth wheel in the car of development'. The primary explanation for the relative lack of attention given to the field of C4D is the difficulty of attributing development outcomes directly to the media. As one project officer from a leading bilateral donor agency said recently, 'we won't fund anything that doesn't have a straight [causal] line'. This problem is compounded by the lingering perception in some contexts that media are somehow peripheral, or at least non-essential, to the 'real' work of development.

The C4D community's effort to raise their profile produces much discourse highlighting the potential benefits that media can have for development. As Nobuya Inagaki (2007: 1) puts it, 'one of the ways to turn around the marginalized status of communication in development efforts is to demonstrate the positive impacts of communication on development initiatives'. However, this 'positive' approach may have unintended consequences. Presenting media, and particularly information and communications technologies (ICTs), as a magic bullet for development has also become a key feature of the discourse of many corporations involved in international development. As is argued in Chapter 1, it allows them to frame their interventions as technical, apolitical projects which draw attention away from the structural causes of poverty and inequality, in which they could be implicated. But new communication technologies and media in general are not a panacea for development. They cannot bring about development by themselves and, as Chapter 1 explains, they can even contribute to the exacerbation of inequalities. If raising the profile of media in development is achieved at the expense of cultivating a critical understanding of the role of media, then it is, in my view, a dangerous agenda which may serve more than just the interests of the C4D community.

Media development Media development refers to in-country and donor-led initiatives designed to develop the media sector within a specific region or country. As Chapter 3 makes clear, these include efforts aimed at promoting independence, plurality, professionalism, capacity, an enabling environment, economic sustainability and media literacy. The distinction between media development and C4D is that the focus in media development is on developing the media, rather than on using media as a mechanism for achieving other development outcomes.

Despite some progress in recent years, the field of media development still remains in its infancy, particularly compared to C4D. Linje Manyozo (2011: 321), for example, argues that dominant C4D theories and discourses treat issues relating to media development – including the role of the media in democracy and good governance – either as a 'footnote' or overlook them entirely. Indeed, it is estimated that USAID spends four times more on C4D-related projects than it does on media development (CIMA 2013a). Overall, only around 0.5 per cent of all international development spending is related to media development (Nelson and Susman-Peña 2012). Moreover, Mark Nelson and Tara Susman-Peña (ibid.: 8) describe spending in this area as 'haphazard … random …, poorly coordinated with broader reforms and rarely led by the countries that are receiving the assistance'. Elsewhere Susman-Peña (2012: 36) adds that 'most international donors do not recognize media development as a development sector in its own right'.

It is in this context that Chapter 3 provides readers with an all-too-rare critical introduction to this neglected but important field by reviewing the multiple, contested and often rather confusing ways in which media development is defined, measured and practised. The underlying argument is that confronting the conceptual confusion surrounding this issue is necessary both for enhancing the status of this field and improving the effectiveness of interventions in this area. Building on this discussion of what media development *is*, Chapter 4 addresses the question of how it might contribute to development. Specifically, this chapter critically reviews the claims and evidence that link media development to good governance, democracy and economic development. It also considers broader accounts of the intrinsic value of media development and the functions of community media. The overall argument is that efforts to high-light the importance of media development should exist along-side, rather than seek to obscure, recognition of the complex and multiple roles that media have in development. Ultimately, it is not helpful to pretend that the lines of causality between media development and development are direct and linear.

Media representations of development The study of media representations of development is concerned with the content, causes and consequences of media representations of both development and the global South, as they are communicated to audiences in the global North. This includes everything from humanitarian appeals and international news coverage, to novels, feature films and reality television programmes set in foreign countries.

Unfortunately, this subject is also largely regarded as 'peripheral to the "real work" of development' (Smith and Yanacopulos 2004: 658). This marginalization persists in spite of the fact that the arguments linking representations of development to development itself are compelling. The literature from both media studies and development studies contends that media coverage is heavily implicated in public perceptions of development and the global South and that this in turn has real-world consequences – for ethical consumerism, public policy, charitable donations and support for NGOs, among other things. It also highlights the way in which the appearance of the global South in the media reinforces (or otherwise) global power relations between the North and South – which is itself another 'significant element of the politics of development' (ibid.: 659).

In this context, Chapters 5 and 6 aim to draw attention to the important role of media representations in development, while at the same time maintaining a critical perspective. Chapter 5 critically reviews dominant strategies of humanitarian communication used by NGOs, including images and narratives associated with 'shock effects', 'deliberate positivism' and post-humanitarian communication. The implications of new media are also discussed. The overall argument is that there is no ideal form of NGO appeal, only alternative responses to the broader tensions inherent within humanitarian communications. Chapter 6 discusses how Western media coverage in general might be implicated in international development, specifically regarding its possible impact on overseas aid budgets, the formation of cosmopolitan sentiments and global relations of power. Once again, the overall point is that while media (representations) do matter for development, explaining and evidencing precisely *how* media matter is far more challenging than is often pretended.

Integrating media studies and development studies

Considerations of the role of media representations of develop-ment very rarely take place alongside discussions of C4D and media development. This book will demonstrate the advantages of giving equal weight to each of these three fields and to dis-cussing them together. In particular, the conclusion of this book will draw out how this helps to challenge common assumptions about the range of actors involved in development, where devel-opment takes place, how to conceive of the role of media and the value of a political economy perspective. It will also show how concepts common to media studies – such as mediation, mediatization, immediacy, hypermediacy and re-mediation – can be useful for development studies, and vice versa.

More generally, bringing these three fields together in one place will help to show that a range of perspectives is now neces-sary to fully understand the multifaceted nature of contemporary phenomena. *Makutano Junction*, for example, is a Kenyan soap opera designed primarily to promote change in audience knowledge, attitude and behaviour. As such, we might describe it as an example of a particular form of C4D. Yet it has also played a major role in the development of the Kenyan entertainment television industry, which makes it relevant to the field of media development. Furthermore, this soap opera has also been used as a resource for global citizenship lessons in secondary schools in the UK and eastern Europe, thus making it relevant to media representations of development. The implications that *Makutano Junction* has for international development therefore spread well beyond the boundaries of any one of these three fields.

Similarly, the Commonwealth Broadcasting Association (CBA), which is the largest global association of public service broadcasters, promotes public service media around the world through information sharing, training, research and partnerships. We might, therefore, consider it most appropriate to discuss it in terms of its contribution to media development. Yet it also supports the production of media coverage of development through its WorldView fund and it is involved in several C4D projects in Pakistan and in the Pacific. The theoretical frameworks we might want to apply to the activities of organizations like the CBA and projects like *Makutano Junction* cannot be found in any one subject area. Only by bringing together the disciplines of media studies and development studies – starting with these three particular fields – can we develop a more sophisticated understanding of international development in an increasingly mediatized world.

Defining media and development

It is worth dwelling briefly upon the key terms that will be used throughout this book. Unfortunately, the terms 'media' and 'development' defy easy definition. Within the field of C4D, for example, understandings of development shift between a narrow focus on targeted, measurable change in audience knowledge, attitude and practice (brought about by external change agents), to change that is unpredictable and driven by people themselves. Alongside these two views of development, understandings of the role of media shift from their being seen as instruments for delivering messages to being seen as a means of facilitating two-way, horizontal dialogue. In contrast to both of these perspectives, in the field of media development, the media are understood more as an institution, acting upon and in concert with many other institutions in society. In this approach, the media are implicated, not necessarily in individual behaviour change or collective empowerment, but in aspects of democracy, good governance and economic growth. Finally, when considering media representations of development, we are far more inclined to think of media in terms of their contribution either to public support for the activities of development actors based in the global North, or to the circulation of discourses and how this contributes to global relations of power. It should be clear, therefore, that understanding the relationship between media and development requires careful handling of two very slippery terms.

It is important to be aware, not only that meanings of 'development' can stretch from a concern for modernization (Chapter 1) and/or economic growth (Chapter 4) to an expansion in freedoms (Chapter 4), but that efforts to promote well-being in the name of development are often unsuccessful. Moreover, development interventions have also been accused of actively exacerbating poverty and inequality. A central claim of post-development literature is that 'processes of modernity, in particular industrialisation, urbanisation and the weakening of communal ties, have led to a massive increase in new forms of poverty that have been worsened by schemes of "development" such as poverty reduction strategies' (Shaffer 2012: 1772).

The point is that media's contribution to development is not only multifaceted, but that it may not always be a 'good' thing. Even if media can make positive contributions to development, this is not necessarily the same as reducing levels of poverty and inequality.

This book is concerned with the role of media, specifically, rather than the role of communication in general, in development. On the one hand, this establishes a rather narrow focus, since media are clearly only one possible form of communication. Other forms of communication, such as theatre, interpersonal communication and indigenous knowledge communication systems (IKCS), also have a very important role to play in development (see Manyozo 2012: 95). On the other hand, choosing to focus on the media is helpful for drawing our attention, not only towards examining different ways of communicating for development, but also towards examining the practices and politics of the dominant institutions involved in communicating about development. As Karin Wilkins and Florencia Enghel (2013: 178) argue,

> Most of our communication research in development focuses on how communication works *for* social change in the implementation of programs, privileging applied over critical work. But ... the public relations aspect of development as an industry [also] merits our critical scrutiny. This approach to development is not just a matter of public relations for aid expenditures, it also endorses technological optimism in the power of digital media and individual actions. As in many emerging and privatized development enterprises, success can be considered beyond specific project outcomes, toward promoting the latent values that legitimate the agenda of private global industry in the service of the neoliberal project.

Given that media appear to play an increasingly pervasive role in many societies, Wilkins and Enghel are right to argue that the industries involved in communication certainly merit our critical scrutiny.

Finally, to be clear, the main focus of this book is on critically reviewing, within a development context, different ways of understanding the role of media, rather than distinguishing between the roles of different technologies. While it is of course important to understand the relative strengths and weakness of radio compared to television, or short message service (SMS) compared to posters, for example, such considerations assume a much greater significance once we have established what we think media can and cannot do, under what circumstances and in relation to different understandings of development. Put another way, the question of whether television or radio is a more suitable means of communicating development messages about HIV/AIDS, for example, fails to engage with the more fundamental question of whether using media as a tool for communicating development messages is the most appropriate approach in the first place. I would argue that in most cases it is not.

Having said this, it is difficult to ignore the increasingly widespread claims that new technologies have the capacity to transform international development. Therefore, particular consideration is given throughout to whether new technologies force us to entirely rethink how we understand media's relationship with development, or whether they remain largely compatible with models applied to 'old' media. In line with the broader aim of this book, though, the emphasis throughout is on challenging celebratory claims about the seemingly enormous potential of new technologies for international development. Techno-optimist discourses are helpful only to the vested interests they serve – they certainly do not assist in my aim here to produce considered understandings of the role of media.

The key ambition of this book is to highlight the increasing importance of the media in development, while at the same time emphasizing the varieties, complexities and contingencies of its role. As media increasingly infiltrate our lives and appear to help shape the world around us, I hope this book will go some way towards enabling us to better understand the implications of this for the persistence of poverty and inequality around the world.

1 | Media for Development: Magic Bullet or Corporate Tool?

Perhaps the most apparent role for media in development is as a channel for delivering information to the public. It is not difficult to appreciate how media, whether through posters, television advertisements or SMS, can act as an important source of information for individuals regarding all manner of development-related issues, such as family planning, nutrition and HIV/AIDS prevention.

This particular function of the media is referred to as a media *for* development (M4D) approach; defined here as the strategic use of the media as a tool for delivering positive change in individuals' knowledge, attitude and practice in order to achieve development results. The aim of an M4D project is to design the most appropriate message, targeted at the most relevant audience, delivered through the most suitable media channels in order to promote desirable change in a particular behaviour.

Rather than focusing on the historical legacy of this particular approach, which can be found elsewhere (Waisbord 2000; Melkote and Steeves 2001), the aim of this chapter is to clearly set out its key defining features so that readers can better identify contemporary examples of this approach. To help achieve this, reference is made throughout to the work of a particular high-profile current example of M4D work; that of Development Media International (DMI). DMI is a UK-based social enterprise, which describes itself as '[delivering] mass media campaigns to change behaviours and save lives in developing countries' (DMI 2013a). Its focus is primarily on changing behaviours related to reproductive, maternal, newborn and child health, largely in Africa and Asia.

As well as enabling readers to recognize examples of M4D projects, this chapter also equips readers with a critical perspective on this approach. This is crucial as M4D (and its variants) is often presented entirely unproblematically, particularly in relation to new information and communications technologies (ICTs). The results of a meta-analysis of all academic articles which addressed the topic of communication and development between 1998 and 2007 found that 'rather than disappear from the literature, it seems there has been a resurgence of the use of this paradigm, either explicit or implicit, as fully 37.3 percent of the articles made use of this frame for their research' (Ogan et al. 2009: 661).

Christine Ogan and her colleagues (ibid.: 656) conclude their analysis by suggesting that 'perhaps the introduction of ICTs into the discourse of development has caused some scholars to forget that technology cannot provide a magic multiplier effect for the poorest of the poor'. Indeed, their results also show, rather worryingly, that only 20 per cent of all articles were critical of any of the communication paradigms used to frame development.

In order to help combat this pervasive and uncritical (though not unchallenged) embrace of the M4D approach, this chapter also provides a clear overview of its various limitations. The central argument is that while the M4D approach certainly has the capacity to promote a particular kind of development (associated with individual behaviour change), under certain conditions, as with any intervention, there are inevitable limitations, assumptions and blind spots that need to be recognized. Moreover, the M4D approach can also be accused of helping to reinforce the agenda of large corporations involved in international development, particularly when applied to ICTs.

The final section of this chapter recognizes that, in practice, media-related development projects can look very different to the ideal form of M4D discussed and critiqued here. It therefore outlines two particular hybrid forms of M4D that, to varying degrees, incorporate the strategies and objectives of other approaches.

Defining features of the M4D approach

1 Information provision The central feature of the M4D approach is that information acquisition by individuals is understood to be a vital part of the development process. The essential problem is taken to be a lack of (appropriate or accurate) information regarding a particular issue, such as being unaware of free healthcare services or the necessity for climate change adaptation. The solution to this problem, then, is to combat such (apparent) ignorance by providing individuals with relevant information, which, it is predicted, will result in desirable behaviour change.

The central role of information and behaviour change in the M4D approach is made explicit in the way DMI describes its core activities.

> We design and deliver radio and TV campaigns that are designed to improve health outcomes by informing people about important healthcare issues and promoting behaviour change where appropriate … If a mother can recognise that her baby has diarrhoea and is able to provide her child with oral rehydration therapy, then the child is far more likely to reach the age of five. (DMI 2013a)

In this formula, in which information is linked directly to individual behaviour change, the mass media are usually seen

as the most effective mechanism for delivering the relevant information. Unlike conventional, classroom-based, education, the
mass media can reach relatively very large numbers of people,
very quickly, repetitively and inexpensively. Radio in particular
is often cited as being especially effective in many contexts, not
least because radio audiences are not required to be literate.
DMI (ibid.) justify their focus on the mass media on precisely
these grounds, arguing that

> In Africa, the most popular media is radio, because of its
> lower cost and portability: for example, in Uganda, 74% of the
> population listen to the radio at least once per week (compared
> to 11% for TV). On average, it is between 100 and 1,000 times
> more cost-effective to use radio and television than face-to-face
> 'community-level' channels, such as street theatre.

More recently, though, mobile phones are increasingly being
used as the mechanism for delivering information. One example
of this is the work of the Mobile Alliance for Maternal Action
(MAMA), which is a public–private partnership that provides
mobile health messages primarily to pregnant women and new
mothers, either through SMS or voice messages. An example
of a MAMA SMS reads as follows: 'a cord infection can make
your baby very ill. Sponge the cord with clean water and leave
it uncovered to dry. It needs nothing else.'

2 Cultivating appropriate attitudes Alongside the need to deliver appropriate information, an M4D approach also commonly
includes a focus on the importance of developing suitable attitudes. This emphasis on attitudes stems from the work of Max
Weber (1930) and Daniel Lerner (1958), who both argued that
the development of a society depends upon the predominance of
a 'modern', rather than a 'traditional', mental outlook; characterized as being rational, calculating and forward-thinking.

Few would now refer to individuals as having either modern or traditional mental structures or make claims about the 'backwardness' of some cultures compared to others (see Rogers 1969). Yet the belief that culture and individual attitudes are a key determinant of development remains – in the global North as well as the South. For example, one of the key drivers of deprivation and social exclusion in the North Earlham, Larkman and Marlpit (NELM) housing estates in the city of Norwich, UK (one mile from the University of East Anglia), is often claimed to be a lack of aspiration as well as entrenched (resistant) attitudes towards the local authorities (Rogaly and Taylor 2009). Indeed, the establishment of the community radio station – Future Radio – here in 2004 was designed, at least initially, to tackle this perceived 'sub-culture' (Rogers 1969).

If an individual's attitude is taken as a key driver of (or obstacle to) development, then one function of the media in this scenario is to challenge traditional norms and values and instead develop a modern or more appropriate outlook. This is revealed in the work of DMI (2013a), when they state, for example, that

> Cultural and social factors can also prevent people from changing their behaviours. For example, a belief that leprosy is caused by a divine curse rather than by bacteria, and the social stigma that is attached to it as a result, prevents people from coming forward for treatment ... We address whatever the barriers are to a particular behaviour change in a given country; if cultural issues are important, as they often are, then we will tackle these alongside simply imparting knowledge.

This statement makes clear that, in the M4D approach, culture is often understood as a barrier to development, and not as an 'ally' of development or part of a 'way of life', as in alternative approaches to media and development (see Tufte 2008: 330).

3 Assumptions about communication, audiences and behaviour change A third feature of the M4D approach is its basis in a combination of mutually reinforcing theories from media studies, social psychology and diffusion studies (the study of how innovations spread through society) (Sparks 2007: 26). Theories from media studies, and the 'two step flow' (Katz and Lazarsfeld 1955) model of communication in particular, are used to explain how information and ideas are transferred from media to individual members of society. The two step flow model suggests that information flows from media to the general public in two stages – first, from media to opinion leaders or local elites (who have the resources to access and respond to the information), and secondly, from such opinion leaders to the masses – through interpersonal communication (i.e. talk). The key emphasis in this two step flow model is the importance of targeting opinion leaders and of combining communication through media with interpersonal communication. These two ideas remain an important feature of most M4D interventions today, even if the two step flow model itself is not explicitly cited.

This emphasis on the importance of talk in behaviour change and the disaggregation of different target audiences has replaced the widely discredited 'hypodermic needle' model of communication, which asserts that mass media have a direct and powerful effect on passive audiences. Inherent in both of these models, though, and in the M4D approach more generally, is the assumption that communication is a largely linear, unidirectional process in which information is sent from 'senders' to 'receivers' through particular channels.

Theories from diffusion studies reinforce the basic premises of the two step flow model of communications. In particular, Rogers' (1962) widely cited theory of 'diffusion of innovations' suggests that new innovations spread throughout society in a relatively predictable pattern, with the early adopters of new innovations having a tendency to be elites. After an innovation has subsequently spread among the majority of the population, the last members of society to adopt will be the 'laggards', characterized by Rogers as having a focus on traditions.

Rogers' theory of diffusion characterizes the adoption of innovations as an individual decision-making process involving five stages: awareness, knowledge and interest, decision, trial, and adoption/rejection. Whereas media are taken to be central to the first stage of the process, Rogers saw 'personal sources' (ibid.: 99) as most important during the later stages of the adoption process. Thus, this model of diffusion also emphasizes the vital role of both interpersonal communication and the differences between groups in society, just as in the two step flow model.

Finally, theories from social psychology are used to help explain how individuals learn and adopt new behaviours, such as condom use or hand washing, based on the experience of media consumption. Some of the most widely cited theories in this context include Social Learning Theory, the Stages of Change Model and the Health Belief Model. In a similar way to Rogers' model of diffusion, the Stages of Change Model, for example, seeks to describe the sequence of stages through which an individual passes in the adoption of a 'positive' behaviour. In this model the stages consist of: *pre-contemplation*, *contemplation* of the reasons to change a behaviour, *preparation* to change a behaviour, *action* and, finally, *maintenance* of that action. The role of communication in this model is targeted at the stage being addressed, so, for example, to help move an individual from *pre-contemplation* to *contemplation*, the role of media might be to raise awareness of the issue and to demonstrate the positive reasons to adopt that behaviour (Prochaska et al. 1992). What characterizes this and other theories of behaviour change, as well as Rogers' theory of diffusion, is that they assume that behaviour change is a product of *individual* psychology (rather than group norms and processes) and that decision-making is a *rational* (rather than emotional) process.

In summary, whether these theories of behaviour change, media effects and diffusion are explicitly cited by M4D projects or not, M4D interventions do all share a set of common assumptions about the nature of communication (as a linear, one-to-many, process), audiences (as relatively passive) and behaviour change (as based on individual, rational, decision-making).

4 Change is planned, controlled, targeted, measurable, predictable and managed by external change agents Another key dimension of the M4D approach is that it requires external change agents (usually foreign consultants) to play a central role in managing the process of change. Colin Sparks (2007: 53) discusses the role and characteristics of change agents in the following way:

> The experts are different from their audience in almost every respect. The experts have intentions as to what sense the audience should make of their messages. The experts set the goals of the programme and design the material it will use ... in order to achieve the results that they themselves have defined ... The experts are communicating something ... of which they are in possession, to people who are ignorant of these insights.

Implicit in this description is the idea that local people are not only ignorant but are also somewhat passive and predictable in the process of development. If the change agent was not there to identify the missing information, design the intervention and ensure it was delivered effectively, change would not otherwise occur.

In the M4D approach, not only is change being driven from outside the community, but the change agent is pursuing a particular kind of change. In contrast to the kind of unpredictable, uncontrolled and wide-ranging social change that characterized the Arab Spring, for example, M4D interventions seek to achieve change that is planned in advance, targeted at particular audiences, limited in scope and aimed at measurable outcomes. This narrow conceptualization of change is most obvious in the ways in which M4D projects are usually evaluated. Implicit in the evaluations described below is the idea that projects aim to achieve certain predetermined outcomes, limited to specific changes in individual behaviours, and that these outcomes can be both accurately measured and attributed directly to the M4D campaign. There is even a claim that the outcomes of such interventions can be accurately predicted in advance.

5 An instrumental view of participation To be clear, although projects adopting an M4D approach may be managed by external change agents and characterized by a sender–receiver model of communication, they are not necessarily imposed on recipient communities without any consultation. If media are to be used effectively as channels for delivering information to audiences with the intention of promoting behaviour change, then it is vital for the messages to be relevant to the particular contexts in which they will be received. Such interventions are much more likely to be effective if they are based on an understanding of what particular cultural beliefs currently prevent individuals from engaging in particular behaviours, for example. Similarly, knowledge of the media consumption habits of the target population will enable them to be reached more effectively. There is little point producing even the most well-made television drama, for example, if the target audience of women in rural areas does not have access to television, is too busy to watch when it is broadcast or doesn't like television dramas.

To achieve this level of understanding of audiences, at least some level of participation from the local community is required, and this must inevitably involve some degree of two-way and horizontal communication. What characterizes the M4D approach, though, is the nature and extent of this participation. Participation of the local community in this approach is fundamentally a *means* to achieving more effective use of media, rather than an *end* in itself. Put another way, the aim of consulting with the target audience, or of employing some local staff, is to maximize the effectiveness and delivery of predetermined messages, rather than to involve communities in determining the problems and the most appropriate courses of action themselves (Waisbord 2000: 10). This instrumental approach to participation is evident in the way in which DMI (2013b: 2) describes the audience research necessary for designing their campaigns.

> A campaign should be preceded by a robust research process, using focus groups and other qualitative techniques to understand what the target audience's key values are, and what the barriers are to behaviour change. This research should then be converted into creative outputs tailored to local values, culture and sensitivities, before being pre-tested using focus groups. Detailed audience research is necessary to ensure that messages are transmitted through the right media and at the right times to reach their target audience.

Evaluating M4D interventions Having identified the five key aspects of an M4D approach, it will be useful to end this overview with a critical review of how M4D are evaluated. Evaluations of M4D projects not only help to reveal a number of the key dimensions of this approach but play a key role in legitimizing it. Such evaluations are commonly conducted in one of two ways. Either the levels of knowledge, attitude and practice of audiences are measured *before* the intervention begins

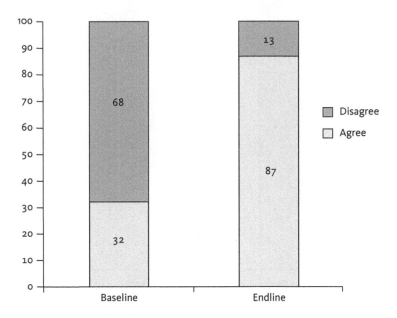

1.1 *Makutano Junction* viewers' response to the notion that 'all parents have the right to become school committee members'

and compared to those *after* the intervention (as in Figure 1.1), or reported changes in the knowledge, attitude and practice of those who *have* been exposed to the relevant media output are compared to those who *have not* (as in Figure 1.2).

Figure 1.1 shows how viewers of the Kenyan entertainment education television soap opera *Makutano Junction* responded to the question 'do all parents have the right to become school committee members?', before and after the relevant series was broadcast. The results appear to show an increase of 55 per cent in the proportion of viewers who knew that all parents do indeed have the right to become school committee members in Kenya. This is signifcant because getting parents involved in local schools is an important part of helping to improve

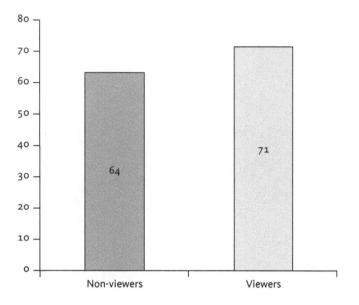

1.2 Percentage of viewers and non-viewers of *Makutano Junction* who claim to own a mosquito net

educational provision. Yet, despite appearances, evidence gained from comparing baseline and endline surveys alone is not sufficient to prove the influence of *Makutano Junction* on levels of knowledge. This approach does not enable us to isolate *Makutano Junction* as the sole cause of the apparent change in knowledge. It may be the case that there were other interventions happening at the time the series was broadcast which may be responsible for changes in knowledge.

Similarly, the data in Figure 1.2 imply that *Makutano Junction* is effective in teaching audiences about the importance of using a mosquito net, because viewers of the soap opera were more likely than non-viewers to claim to own one. However, unless all other possible intervening variables are controlled for, such as age, gender, education level and employment, then we cannot be sure that *Makutano Junction* is the determining factor. It may simply be the case that those individuals who watch *Makutano Junction* are also individuals who are more likely to be predisposed to owning a mosquito net, perhaps because they are better educated, and not necessarily that they are responding to the influence of *Makutano Junction*. Thus, while these measures help us to get closer to isolating the impact of an intervention and are often the best measures available, they are not complete or absolute proof of impact.

There are a number of ways one might seek to ameliorate the problems associated with providing evidence of the effects of M4D campaigns. Multiple regression analysis can be used to control for the influence of other variables and the use of control areas, which are not exposed to the intervention, can also help to isolate the role of media. DMI (2013a), for example, is conducting a randomized controlled trial of its work in Burkina Faso in an effort to 'prove conclusively that we (and we alone) are having the impact on child mortality that we claim'. While its conventional behaviour change campaigns are being broadcast to seven randomly chosen areas within the country, seven other randomized areas are *not* receiving these broadcasts – and are therefore acting as control areas. The media landscape in Burkina Faso provides a rare and ideal opportunity for this trial because its localized media environment means that messages broadcast into intervention areas will not leak into the control areas. Being able to compare control and intervention areas means that differences in behaviour change can be attributed to the intervention, rather than other variables.

This trial in Burkina Faso is being run partly to test the predictions of a model which DMI has developed, which claims to calculate how many lives can be saved by their media campaigns alone, and how much it will cost. This model relies on data from the Lancet Child Survival Series 2003 and 2005, which is used to estimate how many lives could be saved if coverage of existing interventions, such as exclusive breastfeeding or hand washing, were increased from current levels, in different countries. By combining these predictions with the results of previous DMI behaviour change campaigns, which suggest how effective media can be in achieving behaviour change in these areas, DMI claim to be able to predict the overall level of reductions in child mortality that could be achieved. On this basis they claim that 'after three years, comprehensive campaigns could reduce all-cause child mortality by 10% to 20%, depending on the country's profile' (DMI 2013c: 2), and ultimately that 'if we could conduct campaigns in 10 countries over the next 10 years, we should save 1.1 million lives' (DMI 2013d: 1). On the same basis, they go on to calculate the cost per life-year saved of their interventions to be between $2 and $15 (depending on the country) (DMI 2013a). This is lower than that of any other currently available intervention.

In an increasingly competitive and accountability-based donor environment, such quantitative measurements and linear cause–effect models can be very valuable. Yet they are also not without their problems. June Lennie and Jo Tacchi (2011: xi) suggest that a narrow focus on individual behaviour change and a quantitative, measurement-oriented, approach to evaluation can mean that 'the complexity of culture and the context of development initiatives is not taken into account'. Expanding on this in their more recent work, Lennie and Tacchi (2013: 26) argue that

> Social change is not linear, not predictable, and is always contextual. Effectively understanding social change requires considering broader dimensions of the process, beyond the social to encompass the political, economic and cultural ... It also requires a shift in focus from the impact of particular

interventions on specific groups to changes in wider social and organizational systems. This entails an open, holistic and realistic yet critical approach to development and evaluation that draws on a wide range of related theories, concepts and approaches.

Put simply, while quantitative models may go some way towards isolating the effects of media messages on individual behaviours in the short term, they say little about the longer-term consequences of communication campaigns overall for social change more broadly.

Critiques of the M4D approach

1 The role of social structures One of the major appeals of the M4D approach is that it suggests that governments, NGOs, corporate donors and multilateral institutions can design and deliver communication-based interventions which 'make a difference' in a controlled and measurable way, but which don't provoke social unrest or radical critique (perhaps even of their own interventions). In this scenario, the major questions left to be resolved are simply 'whom to target' and 'how'? But while the appearance of being apolitical may make the M4D approach attractive, as we shall see, it is also the source of several key limitations.

The M4D approach is limited by, and fails to address, social structures The outcomes of M4D-based interventions are severely constrained by the fact that individual behaviour change is limited, not just by a lack of information or traditional attitudes, but by more deep-rooted political, social, institutional and economic constraints. Individuals may know and even be positively predisposed towards having a smaller family size or sending their children to school, for example, but if the society they live in has no social security or they cannot afford to pay the schools' fees, they may be unlikely to change their behaviours. Similarly, you may know that certain healthcare services have recently become free, and you may even have changed your attitude towards the efficacy of non-traditional healthcare, but if you live 50 kilometres from the nearest health centre, such knowledge and attitude cannot easily translate into changes in behaviour. To be clear, media may be able to deliver information to individuals, but information is rarely enough by itself to allow for changes in individual behaviour, without a broader transformation of the many complex social and political processes which determine individuals' lives.

DMI (2013a) responds to this crucial issue in two ways. First, it explicitly recognizes that, for many issues, 'providing information alone is not enough [to change behaviour]' and that information provision through media needs to act alongside broader changes in service provision or policy change: 'We don't broadcast messages in a vacuum. Many (but not all) of the behaviours that we are promoting depend on the availability of services, such as clean water or antibiotics. We work closely with supply-side initiatives to make this happen.'

However, DMI also argue that there *are* a (relatively small) number of 'household behaviours', such as exclusive breastfeeding or improved hygiene, which are not reliant on the availability of healthcare services and so *can* be affected by mass media campaigns alone. It is these household behaviours which DMI chooses to focus on most heavily.

Many people cannot recognise when their child has a potentially dangerous illness, or do not know what to do about it, so many deaths are due to lack of knowledge rather than lack of healthcare services ... In some countries we can reduce child mortality by as much as 20%, just through mass media campaigns. (DMI 2013b: 1)

But by targeting only a narrow range of apparent informative or psychological 'barriers', the M4D approach fails to address the broader structural drivers of poverty and inequality. As Tufte and Wildermuth (2013: 12) put it, 'dissemination of information, on its own, is not sufficient to alter the marginalized position of excluded communities'. Manyozo (2012: 110) elaborates on this point further, with the example that

> If people cannot eat healthy food, the root problem is not just nutritional knowledge – workshops on how to cook food will not solve the problem. The fountain problem could be a lack of land on which to grow vegetables [or] the presence of a corrupt corporate buyer who buys all nutritional foods.

To be clear, the M4D approach is characterized by a very narrow definition of 'development' – associated with individual behaviour change – rather than broader social change involving tackling social structures and the root causes of poverty and inequality. The tension here is between the choice to pursue relatively small-scale, discrete, but nevertheless very important, changes in individual behaviour – or to contribute to a much broader vision of development, associated with empowerment, equality and democracy (see Chapters 2 and 4). Many academics in this field line up squarely behind the latter view. Luis Ramiro Beltran (1976: 19), for example, argued that 'an overall change of the social structure is the fundamental pre-requisite for the attainment of genuinely human and democratic development'. Similar, Manyozo (2012: 110) argues that 'mobilising communities to uptake and adopt new knowledge and technology, do[es] not make sense if the communication interventions do not deal with fundamental causes of inequality that have put communities in such positions'.

From a different perspective, though, it is not difficult to see how one might argue that it is inefficient to devote limited resources to pursuing broad, complex and unpredictable development-related objectives, when the M4D approach claims to be able to produce targeted, measurable and cost-efficient change. At stake here are questions regarding the importance of accountability and cost-effectiveness in aid spending and what development actually means. To adopt the M4D approach is to offer a very particular set of answers to these questions.

The M4D approach can harm local media industries and exacerbate inequalities There is an assumption in the M4D approach that the media are an independent variable, or a politically neutral tool which acts upon society but is not influenced by it. This is somewhat implied in the claim by DMI (2013a), for example, that they 'see media simply as a means of delivering behaviour change'. What this perspective overlooks is that media are bound up within existing power structures, evident in concentrations of ownership and unequal access to media. As Beltran (1976: 19) wrote, 'Communication itself is so subdued to the influence of the prevailing organisational arrangements of society that it can hardly be expected to act independently as a main contributor to profound and widespread social transformations.'

As a result, there are many examples of M4D projects which have been accused (either individually or en masse) of actively harming the local media capacity of the countries they work in – either by reinforcing unequal patterns of media ownership or by distorting the local market. For example, Sarah Cramer and Mustafa Babak (2013) argue that large amounts of investment from Western donors in M4D-based interventions in the Afghan media sector in recent years have, alongside Afghanistan's open licensing regulations, contributed to powerful political and religious figures managing to gain control of many of the outlets. As a consequence, they describe the Afghan media sector as having 'grown along historic tension lines, reinforcing differences rather than bridging them'.

This understanding of the media as a politically neutral tool is also associated with the claim that the M4D approach may actively contribute to the exacerbation of existing inequalities among populations. In most developing countries, access to different media is sharply divided according to gender, ethnicity, rural/urban setting, socio-economic status and many other variables. In Kenya, for example, the difference in average levels of household television ownership in 2008 varied between 76 per cent in Nairobi and just 3 per cent in the North Eastern region (KARF 2008). Similarly, while 68 per cent of households in urban areas owned at least one television, the same was true for just 29 per cent of households in rural areas. As a result, any M4D campaigns broadcast on television in Kenya are inevitably more likely to be watched by particular members of society than others. As Paul Hartmann and his colleagues (1989: 259) put it, information 'tends not to trickle [through society] randomly but flow along established channels defined by the social structure'. The consequence is that those who are already marginalized in society are also the ones least likely to benefit from such interventions.

Referring once again to the work of DMI (2013a), their apparent response to this issue is to work primarily in countries which have high levels of media penetration and a concentrated media environment. This ensures that the content they produce will be regularly listened to or watched by a relatively large proportion of the population. For example, DMI (2013c: 2) report the percentage of men and women who listen to the radio or watch television at least once a week in Angola, Burkina

Faso and Cameroon, where they work, to be 82 per cent, 75 per cent and 73 per cent respectively. These relatively high levels of media penetration, combined with high child and maternal mortality rates, are what determine their decision to work in these countries.

However, we could also conclude from this that M4D campaigns, as an approach to achieving behaviour change, are inevitably less effective in countries where audiences are fragmented, as is increasingly the case, or where media penetration rates are relatively low. Furthermore, it remains the case that it is likely to be the most marginalized groups in Angola, Burkina Faso and Cameroon who do not have access to the relevant media and who are least likely to benefit from the information. Thus, unless concrete steps are taken to address existing inequalities of access, inequalities in health outcomes may expand. For some issues, this apparent compounding of inequalities may be further exacerbated by the fact that some members of society are not only less likely to have access to technology, but are also less likely to be able to act on the information they receive. Even if all members of society were informed, through media, about the benefits of a particular technological innovation, it will likely be those with greater power who are better able to adopt and benefit from it – just as in the 'green revolution' in India. As Sparks (2007: 43) puts it, 'development' can be a precondition for the acceptance of development messages, rather than the other way around.

In summary, while M4D campaigns may appear to produce change without getting involved in the messy business of politics and social relations, the influence of social structures is unavoidable. M4D campaigns not only fail to target social structures but their effects are limited by them and they can end up harming local media industries and exacerbating inequalities because of them.

2 M4D and modernization The second major set of critiques of the M4D approach stem from its origins in the modernization paradigm of development. Beginning after the Second World War and for several decades afterwards, modernization was the dominant way in which development was conceived. The basic idea of this theory was that 'underdeveloped' societies should aim to replicate the political, economic, social and cultural characteristics of 'modern', 'developed', Western societies. This 'evolution' of society referred primarily to processes of industrialization, urbanization, democratization and the use of advanced technologies. These processes were also perceived to rely upon a simultaneous transition from traditional attitudes and values to more modern ones (Lerner 1958). At the time, the mass media were understood to be able to act as 'magic multipliers' (Rogers 1969) – or key drivers of changes in knowledge and attitude. Thus, grand claims were made about the capacity of the mass media to transform societies.

However, this view of development as modernization has been relentlessly and substantially critiqued and undermined, particularly since the 1970s, not least for having a patronizing, one-size-fits-all, and ultimately self-serving, view of development. Advocates of 'another development' (see Servaes 1995) accuse the modernization paradigm of failing to recognize the agency and distinctiveness of local populations and that every society must pursue its own unique path to development. From the perspective of dependency theory, modernization was criticized for actively promoting an oppressive world system in which poorer countries will continue to be exploited by richer countries as long as they continue to pursue closer integration into the world market. As a consequence of these and many other critiques, the dominance of the modernization paradigm of development has been replaced by multiple competing narratives about what development is and how it can be achieved.

Despite its relative decline, though, the modernization discourse of 'progress' still remains highly influential and is implicit in many development policies and interventions today – including the M4D approach.

The M4D approach can promote a Western vision of modernity While contemporary M4D campaigns would not make the same claims about the direct and large-scale transformative capacity of media for all of society, they do remain committed to some dimensions of the modernization paradigm – especially a belief in the superiority of modern over traditional ideas (Sparks 2007: 47). Such an assumption is apparent, for example, in the following description of a DMI video which aims to challenge audiences' traditional beliefs about the cause and cure of leprosy: 'In South Asia ... leprosy is considered by Hindu scripture to be a curse of God. This video featured Nepal's two leading comedians aiming to persuade people that [leprosy] was not only easy to cure [through modern medicine], but also that God had nothing to do with it' (DMI 2013a).

This example also helps to illustrate that it is in the communication of information and norms associated with modern scientific medicine and health practices that this assumption appears most valid. Few would object to the principle of promoting many health behaviours that are rooted in knowledge generated by modern scientific medicine, such as child immunization or nutritional advice. Similarly, cultural beliefs that maintain the practice of female genital mutilation/cutting (FGM/C) are often cited as examples of traditional ideas that are universally unacceptable and should be eliminated.

But while it may be difficult to disagree with the general premise of using media to promote specific attitudes related to health and to challenge certain others, the broader question of whether modern ideas are superior to local or traditional ones, in all contexts, is much more problematic. For example, one of the core aims of the entertainment education soap operas produced by the Population Media Centre is to 'bring about the stabilization of human population numbers ... [by] educating people about the benefits of small families' (PMC 2013). While their overall objectives may be well intended, such an approach faces an unavoidable tension between what it perceives to be a universal norm and women's reproductive rights (see Knudsen 2006). Who decides whose families are too large? Who determines the ideal family size, and on what basis? The dilemmas raised by a commitment to the superiority of modern over traditional ideas are summed up well by Silvio Waisbord (2005: 90) in the following passage:

> Who ha[s] the right to determine which cultural practices
> are desirable and need to be preserved? ... When is universal-
> ism defensible? Does relativism always trump universalistic
> principles? What if communities invoke cultural sovereignty
> to defend practices that are widely contrary to other people's
> (particularly Northern) norms? ... Upon what grounds should
> we defend cultural identity while aiming to change sexual and
> marriage practices rooted in paternalistic cultures?

If interventions are supply-led rather than demand-driven, as M4D projects often are, they may fail to recognize that what is appropriate in one society may not be so appropriate in another, or that the most pressing development needs of the population may actually be very different from the ones identified by external change agents. Moreover, given that it is almost exclusively ideas produced and accepted within the West which are disseminated by (largely Western-based) M4D campaigns, it is possible to understand how some M4D campaigns might still be accused of promoting modernization, or a Western model of development. As Claude Alvares (1992: 230) puts it, 'knowledge is power, but power is also knowledge. Power decides what is knowledge and what is not knowledge.'

The M4D approach fails to recognize or utilize the agency of audiences A second critique of the M4D approach, linked to its foundations in the modernization paradigm, concerns its implicit assumptions about the audience. The models of behaviour change which the M4D approach relies upon generally imply a passive and ignorant audience which, as long as the message is suitably designed, will respond predictably and positively to a campaign. This is evident in the following, rather striking, account by Gareth Locksley (2008: 8) of the apparent role of media in behaviour change.

> Belief in the media's ability to influence behaviour is evidenced by the amounts spent on global advertising – totalling about $400 billion in 2005 ... This large sum is targeted at influencing behaviour so it is safe to assume that the behavioural influence is valid. The storyline is simple: the media can contribute to development by bringing about beneficial changes in the behaviour of individuals, groups, and organizations. Whether the media bring about change depends on its content, tailoring to target audiences, and, to some degree, its interactivity.

I contend that the 'storyline' of media effects is anything but simple. Large amounts of spending on advertising are evidence only that media are assumed to play some role in public consumption habits – not that media necessarily have powerful and direct effects on what all audiences do, as Locksley implies. Moreover, it is not difficult to appreciate that the effects that media have on audiences depend on far more than how well designed and targeted the content is. Audience research in media studies consistently makes clear that audiences are active in the negotiation of the meaning of media content (Barker 1999).

Within any group of audience members, each individual will respond differently to an M4D campaign (or any media text), depending on the context in which they consume it and their own personal background, beliefs, education and experiences. As a result, they may ignore it, laugh at it, misunderstand it, talk over it or interpret and respond to it in any number of alternative ways. Similarly, as active audiences, their future behaviour in relation to the subject matter of the campaign will be a function, not only of their active response to the content, but also of their willingness and ability to negotiate the social, cultural, economic and political conditions in the society in which they live (as discussed above). To claim, as Waisbord (2005: 83) does, that 'the path from information to attitude to practice does not run straight' is to put it mildly.

The purpose of emphasizing the active nature of the audience here is not to argue that M4D campaigns may not have some effect on the knowledge, attitude and behaviour of individuals. Rather, it is to suggest that the reasons why publics may change their behaviours, and the role that media play in those changes, are considerably more complex, contingent and unpredictable than is often claimed. Put another way, it may indeed be the case that a certain percentage of a population has adopted a changed behaviour during the time that an M4D campaign has run. But to suggest that this is a direct consequence of audiences passively and predictably absorbing the messages sent to them, and rationally deciding to change their behaviours in response, would be to deny those individuals their very real agency in making up their own minds, and the complexities and contingencies of their decision-making. It is the suggestion that audiences in the global South are, at least to some extent, passive and predictable which links contemporary M4D campaigns to the modernization paradigm. There is little room for self-determination in an M4D approach.

Furthermore, if we accept that audiences are active, critical, imaginative and often resistant in their consumption of media texts, might there not be equally valuable, if not more valuable, alternative ways of making use of media to facilitate development, rather than using these technologies only as channels for information delivery? This question is explored in more detail in Chapter 2. For now, though, it should be clear that we might take issue with the M4D approach on the grounds that it can be used to promote a Western vision of modernity that may not be appropriate in all contexts and that it fails to recognize or utilize the agency of audiences.

The importance of a critical perspective on M4D Recognizing the various criticisms discussed here is clearly important for understanding what an M4D approach can and cannot achieve and how such projects should be designed and implemented. Yet there are also two other reasons why it is important to adopt a critical perspective regarding M4D. First, since an M4D approach is increasingly being adopted within the rapidly expanding field of 'information and communications technologies for development' (ICT4D), it is important to ensure that the lessons learnt over the last thirty years regarding the failures, limitations and blind spots of this approach are not forgotten. The field of ICT4D is concerned with the application of ICTs, including the internet and mobile phones, to development goals. In academia, a recent study (Ogan et al. 2009) found that more than half of all journal articles addressing the topic of communication and development between 2004 and 2007 focused primarily on ICTs. Moreover, 45 per cent of those ICT-related articles situated their research within the modernization paradigm (and 27 per cent were guided by no paradigm at all). Ogan and her colleagues (ibid.: 656) conclude their analysis by arguing that

The more recent attention to ICTs has to do with the constant search for the magic solution to bringing information to people to transform their lives ... Despite years of research that tells us that information is necessary but insufficient to bring about this change, ICTs have become the most recent iteration of the holy grail for development ... Furthermore, because of the appeal of the modernization paradigm, there is a tendency to forget that it cannot work.

Indeed, it is revealing that the articles which used ICT4D as the primary development strategy were far more likely to consider media as the 'prime mover' of development (90 per cent), rather than as a complement to other factors or as having a minimal role.

Claims about the 'magical potential' (Chakravartty 2009: 37) of 'high-tech innovations' to transform the lives of individuals and communities across the global South are also particularly evident in discourses produced by private companies whose philanthropic foundations are involved in international develop-ment. Examples include the Bill and Melinda Gates Founda-tion, Google.org and foundations arising from eBay (Omidyar Network and the Skoll Foundation). In a review of private funding for media and development, Anne Nelson (2009: 8) points out that 'One enormous factor in the growth of "media for development" has been the emergence of a new generation of foundations grounded in new media ... The Gates Foundation may not have invented "media for development," but in recent years it has undoubtedly helped to set the agenda.'

Secondly, it is worthwhile thinking critically about why an M4D approach appears to be so popular in the first place, particularly among private philanthropic foundations. The M4D approach can easily be used to justify private donors providing subsidized access to ICTs in the global South – so that everyone can benefit from the resulting access to information. Yet a focus on providing access to new technologies – or bridging the 'digital divide' – can also be interpreted as a mechanism for allowing corporations to establish new channels of market penetration. It is in this context that Gumucio-Dagron (2008: 77) describes ICTs as 'the point of the lance … of the expanding wave of mercantilism … In the name of "digital divide" great business is being made.'

Furthermore, in the M4D approach the structural forces which shape inequality are obscured and underdevelopment is attributed instead to individual psychological deficiencies. As a result, the M4D approach can be used to draw attention away from consequences of global capitalism and neoliberalism and to place the responsibility for poverty firmly on the individual. From this perspective, governments are no longer at fault for not providing adequate healthcare, for example, and multi-national corporations are not to blame for the externalities of global capitalism. Instead, we are encouraged to rely upon the philanthropy and technical fixes of private companies as the most effective means of promoting development.

Finally, corporations can use the seemingly measurable and directly attributable impacts of an M4D approach as evidence of their successes in delivering a public good. This evidence can be used to offset criticisms of their other corporate practices – for not paying taxes or fair wages, for example (Wilkins and Enghel 2013: 179).

In these and other ways, we might argue that the seemingly neutral, apolitical, nature of the M4D approach and its conceptualization of change as direct and measurable may help to '[advance] the agenda of private global industry in the service of the neoliberal project' (ibid.: 178). As Anita Gurumurthy and Parminder Jeet Singh (2009: 1) suggest, 'the principal ICTD opportunity is to deploy ICTs in order to universalise market fundamentalism in all facets of life'. Whereas the depoliticization of development in the 1970s was accused of serving imperial ambitions and ideological purposes related to the Cold War (see Sparks 2007), in the modern day the same depoliticization can instead be linked to the service of capitalism and a neoliberal ideology.

Whether readers are sympathetic to this particular perspective, or not, it should nevertheless be clear that the M4D approach is far more problematic than it often appears. In response to some of these critiques, the M4D approach has incorporated the strategies of other approaches to create new, hybrid, forms – as we shall now see.

M4D hybrids

While the key dimensions of M4D projects were defined earlier in this chapter, that framework does not fully capture the wide range of practices going on in this area. As James Dean (cited in Alcorn et al. 2011) suggests,

> Media for development is characterized as top-down selling
> of media to individuals. That's a caricature. Many media for
> development projects I've been involved in have tended to focus
> on voice as much as message, building platforms to speak out
> as much as selling a particular product.

Dean is right to argue that many media-related projects that have a focus on behaviour change, and which we might be inclined to characterize as adopting an M4D approach, actually contain multiple objectives. Two of the most common hybrids of the M4D approach are those that incorporate objectives associated with either media development or media advocacy.

Media development hybrids Although DMI was cited frequently above as a 'model' example of an M4D project, it seeks to do more than simply deliver messages. Their approach is to provide training and build the capacity of the Ministry of Health and local media organizations in exchange for free or heavily subsidized airtime for their campaigns. This not only means that the costs of their campaigns are kept low, but that the additional costs of conducting further campaigns on other issues are minimal. It also means that broadcasters can continue to produce their own materials in the long term when the intervention from DMI ends (DMI 2013a). In this way, it also makes a contribution to the development of the media sector in the country – or media development.

But while such capacity-building approaches may enhance the sustainability of M4D-based projects, to be clear, their focus is on enhancing the media's capacity to deliver more of the same kind of interventions. The fundamental aim – to use media only as a vehicle for individual behaviour change – remains.

There are, however, many examples of projects which seek to combine effective behaviour change communication with a broader contribution to media development. *Makutano Junction* is such an example. The primary aim of this Kenyan weekly drama series has always been to use entertaining storylines to deliver relevant and practical information to large audiences. However, since it was established, it has also aimed to contribute to building the capacity of the entertainment television industry in Kenya. Many of the actors, editors, script writers and directors trained and mentored for work on *Makutano Junction* have gone on to take key roles in the production of other similar television and radio dramas in the country. Kenya now has a relatively strong entertainment television industry, and *Makutano Junction* appears to have played an important part in this.

But while this example may help to illustrate that the outcomes of M4D projects can extend to other sectors of the media, it is important to recognize that their contribution to media development still takes a particular, limited, form. Supporting the development of an enabling legal environment in order to sustain press freedom, for example, would require long-term, coordinated and strategic investment involving multiple stakeholders. This is usually beyond the capacity of organizations focused largely on using media to design and deliver development messages.

Media advocacy hybrids Many media-related development projects take seriously the idea that information alone is not enough to change behaviours. They seek to combine an information-based approach with an approach aimed at creating a more favourable social, political and economic environment for behaviour change. Attempts to prevent early marriage, for example, may be more effective if an individual-centred behaviour change campaign is combined with a media-led advocacy campaign to change the legal age of marriage (and to encourage the enforcement and social acceptability of such a law). Facilitating the creation of such an enabling environment generally involves the strategic use of media to put pressure on policy-makers – an approach referred to as media advocacy (Wallack and Dorfman 1996). Such pressure can come either from using media to mobilize community groups or by attempting to influence news coverage of particular issues.

The duel aim of contributing to both individual behaviour change and to broader societal change is implied in many contemporary models of development communication, to varying degrees. Adam Smith International, for example, describes its vision of effective development communication as having the objectives of not only 'providing information' and 'changing

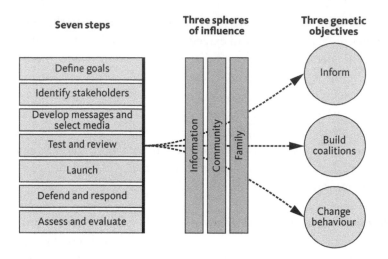

1.3 Adam Smith International's approach to development communication (ASI 2013a)

behaviour', but also of 'building coalitions' (see Figure 1.3). It defines development communication as 'the art and science of making people aware of the benefits of change and of facilitating that change through raising awareness, understanding, and dialogue among stakeholders' (ASI 2013b). Its focus on information and behaviour change reveals its adherence to a conventional M4D approach, while its additional focus on 'dialogue with stakeholders' and 'building coalitions' signals its broader intention to engage with wider structural processes.

This recognition that behaviour change requires more than information being delivered to individuals is also implied in their model by the reference to three 'spheres of influence' – the information, community and family 'spheres'. At the same time, though, the very idea that their approach to development communication can be summarized and formulated in a technical model involving 'three objectives, three spheres of influence and seven steps' (ibid.) is characteristic of a pre-structured, expert-led, approach. In particular, their 'seven steps' implies a one-time, linear model of project implementation that can be made applicable to any context. Thus, despite references to 'dialogue', 'reform' and 'building coalitions', we might conclude that Adam Smith International's model appears still to be tied very closely to a conventional M4D approach. Robin Mansell (1982) and Linje Manyozo (2012) may well describe this as an example of the 'superficial revisionism' of the M4D approach, which has come to characterize the field of communication for development.

The South African-based entertainment education project Soul City provides a useful contrasting example. In his analysis of Soul City, Thomas Tufte (2008: 331) describes their approach as combining 'excellent social marketing strategies' with additional components that 'promote dialogue, challenge power structures and promote community based action'. The most famous example of the apparent impact of its advocacy work comes from its focus on violence against women in its fourth series in 1999. The *Soul City* 4 campaign used its popular standing and authoritative public profile to overtly lobby the main policy actors in this area, in collaboration with several local partners. The compelling nature of its programming on this issue also contributed significantly to a groundswell of public opinion at the time, which also put pressure on these policy actors (Panos 2003: 15). An evaluation of the impact of this series concluded that the speeding up of the implementation of the Domestic Violence Act in South Africa can largely be attributed to the intervention (Usdin et al. 2005: 2434). If the Adam Smith International model is potentially an example of the superficial revisionism of the M4D approach, then the example of Soul City shows how an M4D approach can be successfully combined with attempts to challenge social and legal structures in society.

Conclusion

The M4D approach certainly has its place in the arsenal of strategies linking media to development, particularly in the case of health communication. Indeed, the M4D approach continues to be regularly used in the global North in public health information campaigns to address issues such as road safety and smoking. It is also a very appealing approach because it presents itself as logical, apolitical and based on persuasive quantitative evaluations of impact and cost-effectiveness.

However, this approach to media and development, whether applied to television and radio or mobile phones and posters, carries a number of significant problems. In particular, it is limited in the breadth of its ambition – being focused only on promoting individual behaviour change, rather than addressing the deep-rooted social, economic and political structures which shape behaviours. Indeed, its neglect of social structures not only severely limits the impact it can have on most behaviours but may also result in M4D interventions contributing to the advancement of inequalities. There are also a number of assumptions it makes that we might take issue with; about the passive nature of audiences, the superiority of modern ideas over traditional ones, or the top-down and one-to-many view of communications. While the existence of M4D hybrids may ameliorate some of these issues, it should be clear that the M4D approach does not provide a panacea for development.

Such debates about the value and limitations of the M4D approach have recently taken on a greater importance as the use of ICTs for development gathers pace and frequently adopts this approach (even if this is not made explicit). What is at stake in debates over the M4D approach is not just the effectiveness of one form of intervention over another, but the whole idea of what development is, who pursues it and why.

2 | Participatory Communication in Development: More Questions than Answers

One of the defining features of participatory communication is a resistance to 'top-down', prescribed styles of learning. In order to reflect this, this chapter presents the reader, not with a single, rigid, pre-structured narrative, but with multiple and often contradictory accounts of what participatory communication might mean and what role different media may, or may not, play in this. The expectation is that readers will be encouraged to draw their own conclusions about the definition, value and relevance of participatory communication in development. To aid this process, this chapter will also focus on posing 'problems' or questions for the reader to consider, rather than offering any absolute 'answers'. If there *is* an underlying argument to this chapter, it is simply that participatory communication defies singular definition. Participation is, as Shirley White (1994: 16) argued, kaleidoscopic.

> It changes its colour and shape at the will of the hands in which it is held and, just like the momentary image of the kaleidoscope, it can be very fragile and illusive, changing from one moment to another ... [It] is a complex and dynamic phenomenon, seen from the 'eye of the beholder', and shaped by the 'hand of the powerholder'.

It is hoped that the unconventional format of this chapter will itself provoke readers to think critically about the conventions and implications of different forms of communication. However, I accept that it might well frustrate some readers seeking a definitive summary of this subject. This is a risk I consider worth taking, because, as Roger Silverstone (2006: 45) argued, if we don't take risks in communicating, we lose our capacity for independence of thought, judgement and conscience.

What is participatory communication? What is development?

One way of introducing the idea of participatory communication in development is by considering how its understanding of the role of communication stems from a particular view of development. If we accept that modernization or Westernization is not a universal model of progress, equally relevant to all societies in the world (see Chapter 1), then we should be able to appreciate the argument that there are many alternative, equally valuable, ways of living in the world that are different for different communities. As Jan Servaes (1990: 380) puts it, 'each society must attempt to delineate its own strategy to development, based on its own ecology and culture. Therefore, it should not attempt to blindly imitate program and strategies of other countries with a totally different historical and cultural background.' In this context, development can be seen, not as a universal goal, but as 'an integral, multi-dimensional, and dialectic process that can differ from society to society' (Servaes 1989: 32).

Taking this argument on a stage farther, if we accept that what development means is different in different contexts, then it is reasonable to suggest that it should be up to the people in those communities to define their needs and the scope, pace and nature of change, rather than external experts (Sparks 2007: 57).

As Paulo Freire (1970) argues, the individual must form himself rather than be formed. An emphasis on self-determination and local autonomy helps to ensure both that the local community is engaged in the process of change and that the aims, design and implementation of any development projects are fully appropriate and sustainable.

In this context-specific, 'bottom-up', vision of development, media and communication takes on a particular role. Specifically, the role of communication should be, not to disseminate information in order to change individual behaviours, but to facilitate the inclusive expression of communities' needs. Such a process involves communication that is both horizontal and dialogic, rather than vertical and monologic. In other words, communication is understood as a means of facilitating an ongoing, inclusive and multidirectional exchange between equals, rather than as a one-way system of delivery of information from 'one to many'.

In this approach, the *process* of communicating is particularly important. Communication is not seen simply as a tool for achieving a particular objective, but as a means of empowering all members of the community to have their voices heard. Who gets to speak, about what and under what conditions are all questions that need to be considered. If communication is to play a part in enabling communities to express their own needs, then it is vital that it doesn't reinforce existing power relations. Participatory communication must be an inclusive process in which the 'subaltern' (Spivak 1988) – or those who are most oppressed – are able to speak.

In summary, if we start with a particular vision of development as being culturally specific and locally determined, then the role for communication and media is to facilitate inclusive local expression of needs. But while this may be an appealing vision of media and communication's role in development, it leaves us with a number of difficult questions to answer. Who should take responsibility for ensuring that the process of communication is inclusive and empowering? Allowing those in already established positions of power within the community to lead the process will surely only reinforce existing inequalities. Does genuine participatory communication not, therefore, require the intervention of an external facilitator or 'change agent', just as in the M4D approach? But to what extent is this at odds with the idea that the process of change must emanate from the local community? Precisely what role should the external facilitator play and how can they avoid or at least ameliorate the inevitable inequalities in knowledge and power between themselves and the community?

Furthermore, it is often assumed that inclusive community participation will result in consensus over what to do. But what if it does not? Local elites are likely to be most able to set the agenda of development projects and benefit from them. In which case, the role of the external facilitator must surely be to challenge existing power relations within the community in order to ensure that it is the most marginalized who benefit. But will empowering previously marginalized elements of the community not result in tension and discord? Actively empowering women to play a greater role in community decision-making, for example, may well be desirable for inclusive development, but if it goes against local norms and directly challenges the dominant position of men in the community then it is likely to promote conflict. Should we accept such conflict as an inevitable consequence of promoting structural change through participatory communication? Or is this not a risk worth taking, especially when the outcomes of a participatory approach can be unpredictable and difficult to control? If individuals are unwilling to participate in such activities for fear of the consequences, is it ever acceptable to coerce individuals into participating? And while participatory communication may emphasize the importance of local knowledge and aspirations, might there not be limits to how far some indigenous beliefs and practices are valued? Is there a danger of romanticizing community knowledge?

Participatory communication and Paulo Freire

Pedagogy of the oppressed Another possible way of understanding participatory communication in development is through the work of Paulo Freire, which has been hugely influential in this field. Freire was a Brazilian adult educator who developed a critical philosophy of education – referred to as a 'pedagogy of the oppressed' (1970) – based on his experiences of working with poor, illiterate communities in Brazil in the early 1960s. Although his radical pedagogy was originally developed for education, the basic principles, as we shall see, can be directly applied to development communication. It is worth outlining these principles in some detail here as they are often oversimplified or diluted.

The starting point of Freire's argument is a belief in the existence of an unjust social order which produces both the 'oppressed' and the 'oppressors'. One of the principal mechanisms for maintaining this unjust social order is the existence of a particular false consciousness. As Freire (ibid.: 55) puts it, 'the interests of the oppressors lie in changing the consciousness of the oppressed, not the situation which oppresses them; for the more the oppressed can be led to adapt to the situation, the more easily they can dominated'. This false consciousness is described as a structure of thought which blinds the oppressed from critically recognizing the causes of their oppression. One of the consequences of this false consciousness is that the oppressed, instead of striving for genuine liberation, can aim only to become oppressors themselves because they have been conditioned to accept that their only ideal is to resemble the oppressor. A further consequence is the 'fear of freedom', or the fear that transcending their current 'circle of certainty' in pursuit of a more 'authentic existence' may lead to disorder, or 'destructive fanaticism' (ibid.: 17).

In this context, the way to challenge the unjust social order is to seek to advance critical consciousness among the oppressed. Freire refers to this awakening of critical consciousness as a process of *conscientização* or 'conscientization'. The pedagogy of the oppressed which he outlines in his book of the same name is a pedagogy designed to promote conscientization. Two key dimensions of this pedagogy are praxis and problem-posing.

Praxis, problem-posing and the role of media Freire (ibid.: 33) uses the term praxis to refer to a process of 'reflection and action upon the world in order to transform it'. He argues that this process 'makes oppression and its causes objects of reflection by the oppressed, and from that reflection will come their necessary engagement in the struggle for their liberation' (ibid.: 30). Within this process, the two elements of reflection and action are always working together. True reflection, Freire (ibid.: 48) claims, is necessary for overcoming false consciousness and will always lead to action. Equally, action constitutes authentic praxis only when it is based on critical reflection – otherwise, 'action is pure activism'.

The role of communication in this cycle of action and reflection is apparent in Freire's discussion of the importance of dialogue. He argues that critical and liberating dialogue among the oppressed is central to ensuring reflective participation in the act of liberation. Any attempts at liberation which rely upon instruction and monologues, rather than dialogue, will inevitably 'transform them into masses which can be manipulated ... Propaganda, management, manipulation – all arms of domination – cannot be the instruments of their rehumanisation' (ibid.: 47, 50).

But precisely what form should this dialogue take? A second, related, instrument of liberation is a 'problem-posing' dialogue. In this form of communication, open and thought-provoking questions are used to invite participants to reflect critically and collectively on their own experiences in order to unveil the true reality of their oppression and its causes. Once their oppression is revealed through dialogue, it can become a site of action. In this way, a problem-posing dialogue is crucial for driving the cycle of praxis – because it both prompts initial critical reflection and because it subsequently maintains a cycle of action and reflection.

A key dimension of this form of dialogue is the rejection of conventional sources of authority. The teacher, for example, is 'no longer merely the-one-who-teaches, but one who is himself taught in dialogue with the student, who in turn while being taught also teaches. They become jointly responsible for a process in which all grow' (ibid.: 61). Equally, in this approach, authoritative forms of knowledge and experience derive from the everyday lives of participants, rather than prestigious or well-known examples or events that are often alien or artificial.

This problem-posing dialogue stands in direct contrast with a 'banking type' of education in which the role of the teacher is to deposit information into the students' minds, and the only action of the student is to receive, file and occasionally retrieve such deposits. This form of education is characterized by the authority of the teacher over the student and the assumption that students are ignorant and teachers are knowledgeable. Freire argues that this style of education not only leaves no room for developing critical consciousness, but that it actively works against it by encouraging students to passively accept their place in the world and the fragmented view of reality deposited in them.

It is not difficult to see how these contrasting styles of education map on to different approaches to using media and communication in development. Whereas an M4D approach (discussed in Chapter 1) draws very much on a banking type of education, participatory communication should seek to promote a problem-posing dialogue in pursuit of conscientization. The question is, though, what kinds of media, if any, are appropriate for such a participatory, problem-posing style of communication? The tendency of mass media, such as television, billboards and newspapers, to favour one-way communication severely limits their relevance. Instead, such critical dialogue is far better suited to media that are widely accessible and do not require certain levels of expertise, resources or (media) literacy. Such media should be able to promote local group interaction and reflection and should be owned and controlled by the community rather than by the government or elites. Appropriate media may therefore include community radio, suitable forms of video and photography, interactive posters, visual aids, traditional folk media and local materials that might facilitate dialogue such as cloth or clay.

Yet inclusive critical dialogue does not *depend* on the use of media. It may in fact be more likely to occur through interpersonal communication. As Denise Gray-Felder (cited in Gumucio-Dagron 2001: 4) argues, 'every meaningful lesson or belief I've garnered in life came from someone I value explaining the issue to me and involving me in the process of figuring out the solution'. In which case, forms of interpersonal communication traditionally used in the community should be considered central to participatory communication (although they too are embedded in local relations of power). These include storytelling, group meetings, singing, dancing and especially community theatre (see Boal 1979). Media may well provide an important supplement to these forms of communication, but should certainly not automatically be seen as the dominant mode of participatory communication.

Are you on the side of the oppressed or the oppressor? Freire's understanding of development and the associated role of communication is clearly much more radical than the first account of participatory communication discussed above. One, pragmatic, response to Freire's theory would be to suggest that it may simply be too difficult to bring about the proposed change in the structural forces which it targets. Freire's approach is also clearly incompatible with the culture of most formal development organizations. A pedagogy of the oppressed does not lend itself to straightforward measures of impact or cost-effectiveness, or to universal guidelines for designing and delivering interventions. As Anna Colm (2013) asks, 'is it even possible to run participatory projects in the current context of international development, still very much Western-led and tied to logframes, donors and organisational agendas and structures?' In which case, perhaps we should limit our ambitions to more realistic, smaller-scale objectives that can be achieved within existing structural constraints, albeit with a significant degree of involvement from the local community (Sparks 2007).

For those who take a different view and who accept Freire's argument more fully, the implications are extreme. In Freire's account, any effort to transform the situation of the oppressed which doesn't directly address the unjust social order is a 'false charity' which serves to preserve that order. By contrast, genuine solidarity with the oppressed means 'fighting at their side to transform the objective reality which has made them these "beings for another"' (Freire 1970: 31–2). Freire (ibid.: 42–3) further argues that those oppressors who genuinely wish to convert to being in solidarity with the oppressed must re-examine themselves constantly because they almost always bring with them prejudices which work against revolutionary change, such as a 'lack of confidence in the people's ability to think, to want, and to know'. He adds that 'conversion to the people requires a profound rebirth. Those who undergo it must take on a new form of existence; they can no longer remain as they were.'

Thus, there is little room for ambiguity in response to Freire's theory. One cannot be partially or temporarily in solidarity with the oppressed. This point is often lost in contemporary interpretations of Freire's work. But if we accept this point, then readers are left with two very clear questions: (1) to what extent are you sympathetic to Frerie's theory and (2) if you are sympathetic, do you consider yourself to be on the side of the oppressed or the oppressor?

Participatory communication and diffusion

A further way of defining participatory communication is in opposition to a diffusion model of communication (implied in an M4D approach). Table 2.1 summarizes some of the most common comparisons made between these two dominant approaches in development communication. While a diffusion model focuses on the diffusion of information with the aim of promoting behaviour change (see Chapter 1), a participatory approach aims to promote structural change through horizontal communication.

Making this direct comparison is useful for drawing attention to the very real differences in the theoretical foundations and methodological frameworks of the two approaches. It also serves to highlight the assumptions made by each approach

Table 2.1 Key distinctions between diffusion and participatory approaches to development communication (Gumucio-Dagron 2001; Waisbord 2000; Morris 2005; Sparks 2007; Tufte 2008)

	Diffusion model	Participatory model
The 'problem'	Lack of information and inappropriate attitudes	Structural inequalities/power relations
The 'solution'	Information transfer	Participation/ownership
Desired outcome	Behaviour change/change of social norms	Collective action/structural change/conscientization
Definition of communication	Vertical information transfer	Horizontal dialogue
Definition of development communication	Information dissemination via mass media	Grassroots participation via group interaction
Definition of participation	Participation as a means	Participation as an end
Definition of culture	Culture as an obstacle	Culture as a way of life
Definition of the audience	Passive individual receivers of information	Active citizens who are part of a community
Catalyst of change	External change agent	Facilitator/internal community member
Frameworks	Modernization/diffusion of innovations/banking pedagogy	Praxis/social mobilization/liberating pedagogy
Forms of intervention	Social marketing/behaviour change communication	Participatory action research

about the nature of communication, culture, the audience and development itself. Defining participatory communication in relation to what it is not is also perhaps the most effective way of pinning down what we are actually talking about, because the notion of participatory communication is so fluid.

However, this approach to defining participatory communication also carries a number of problems. Primarily, it implies that the two models of communication are mutually exclusive and that they cannot or do not interact. This is not necessarily the case. There is broad recognition that diffusion-based campaigns will not work unless they involve a significant amount of, albeit instrumental, participation of the local community. Such participation is particularly important in the early stages of project design in helping to determine how relevant the proposed aims and methods are within the local context. Similarly, participatory projects often rely upon some form of information delivery and/ or the teaching of skills. Learning the basics of using a video camera and editing a short film, for example, are best taught thorough instruction, rather than problem-posing.

In an analysis of forty-four different development communication projects, Nancy Morris (2005) finds that rather than being 'polar opposites', the diffusion and participation approaches often informed one another – in terms of both their objectives and outcomes. As is argued by Elizabeth McCall (2011: 8), 'In some United Nations organizations there is recognition that successful programme initiatives can merge community dialogue processes with mass media approaches and other forms of informational and motivational communication and advocacy.'

Indeed, in their meta-analysis of academic articles on development communication, Ogan and her colleagues (2009: 661) found that 11.4 per cent of all projects discussed in their sample explicitly combined a modernization with a participatory framework. Morris (2005: 241) concludes her study by arguing that 'the distinction between participatory and diffusion approaches may be justifiably described as a false dichotomy'.

But while we can accept that these two models of communication may occur, to some extent, within the same project, to what extent can they really be fully integrated? Are there not some aspects of participatory communication which are irreconcilable with a top-down, diffusion-based, approach? What might these be? What would Paulo Freire's view on this question be?

Another problem with comparing participatory communication directly with the diffusion model is that it invites us to make an absolute judgement about which is the most appropriate or effective approach. Making such a judgement carries the assumption that either one is inherently or universally preferable to the other. This may not be a particularly helpful thing to do. Just as there are situations where community dialogue is preferable to the imposition of external norms, so there are circumstances where it is more appropriate to use the mass media as a tool to fill genuine and significant information gaps. Waisbord (2000: 21) points out, for example, that for some urgent, short-term issues, such as epidemics and other public health crises, centralized and rapid decision-making may be preferable to the inevitably slower and often conflicting outcomes of a grassroots process. As Morris (2005: 142) puts it, 'what will work in the local environment is not a question of which is the superior approach. It is a question of shaping project goals to community needs and finding the most appropriate means to pursue those goals.'

This understanding of participatory and diffusion modes of communication as complementary rather than contradictory approaches is central to Thomas Tufte and Paulo Mefalopulos's (2009) 'multi-track' model of development communication. Tufte and Mefalopulos (ibid.: 14) argue that 'the participatory communication paradigm does not call for a *replacement* of the basic communication functions associated with information dissemination, but rather broadens its boundaries to include more interactive ways of communicating' (emphasis added). Based on this argument, they outline their multi-track model, which proposes that a different track, or communication approach, should be taken according to the objectives of the initiative, local circumstances and the phase of the project. They conclude that the difference between monologic and dialogic modes of communication should be seen as 'an asset capable of better addressing the complexity of many situations' (ibid.: 15), rather than as a contradiction.

While this multi-track model may be helpful in drawing attention to the relevance of different modes of communication to different contexts, there is a limit to how far even this model is willing to go in suggesting that both modes of communication are equally valid. Tufte and Mefalopulos (ibid.: 15) draw the line at the first phase of a development project, arguing that

> The research phase must always be based on two-way communication methods ... no matter what the purpose or the sector of the intervention ... This greatly reduces the possibility of relying on incorrect assumptions and avoids the risk of alienating relevant stakeholders by leaving them out of the decision-making process. After this phase, approaches of both modes can be used according to the needs and scope of the initiative.

Is it really the case that neither model of communication is 'better' or 'worse' than the other – they are just more or less appropriate in different contexts? Is the adoption of one approach over the other always an entirely pragmatic decision? Might it not also be seen as ideological?

A final reason why it may be problematic to define participatory communication in contrast to a diffusion model of communication is because it masks the significant variations in the ways in which participation is understood. If participation is kaleidoscopic, as White (1994) describes it, rather than a unified model of communication, then surely any single definition of participation will be incomplete. Perhaps a more meaningful way of understanding the concept is by outlining some of the different, 'fragile and illusive' understandings of participation. This is commonly achieved by identifying different categories or typologies of participation.

Tufte and Mefalopulos (2009), for example, identify two major forms of participation as being the 'social movement' perspective and the 'institutional' perspective. In a project-based or institutional perspective, participation is defined as 'the reach and inclusion of inputs by relevant groups in the design and implementation of a development project'. In this case, participation is seen as a tool to achieve a pre-established goal. Within this perspective, Tufte and Mefalopulos (ibid.) identify a further four ways of understanding participation – (1) as a mechanism for ensuring the inclusive provision of services, (2) as a means of gathering input from civil society to pursue advocacy goals, (3) as a way of monitoring the progress of a project or (4) as a way of evaluating a project. In the social movement perspective, participation is defined much more broadly as 'an empowering process involving the mobilization of people to eliminate unjust hierarchies of knowledge, power, and economic distribution' (ibid.: 4). In this perspective, the establishment of participation as an empowering process is itself the goal.

Another way of categorizing different understandings of participation is by creating a hierarchy of interpretations. Sherry Arnstein's (1969) 'ladder of participation', for example (see Table 2.2), lists eight forms of participation – or degree of citizens' power in determining the outcome of a project. Each form of participation is categorized into one of three levels. The premise of this hierarchy is simply that the farther up the ladder you go, the greater genuine involvement participants have in decision-making. Those forms of participation at the bottom of the ladder, such as 'manipulated' and 'therapy' participation, constitute forms of 'non-participation' or contrived practices which may give the illusion of participation but which only involve participants in an attempt to engineer their support for an outcome that has already been determined. 'Informing', 'consultation' and 'placation' are described as 'tokenistic' forms of participation, which, although allowing participants to have some say in the process, do not contain mechanisms which actually ensure that their contributions will influence the outcomes. Finally, those forms of participation at the top of the ladder afford increasing levels of involvement in actual decision-making, ranging from the ability to negotiate with those in power ('partnership'), to having full or majority decision-making power ('citizen control'). While Arnstein recognizes herself that this ladder simplifies the continuum of participatory practices, its value lies both in enabling us to understand that there can be significant gradation of participation and in cutting through some of the rhetoric associated with this idea.

Table 2.2 Arnstein's ladder of participation (Arnstein 1969)

Citizen control	Degrees of citizen power
Delegated power	
Partnership	
Placation	Degrees of tokenism
Consultation	
Informing	
Therapy	Pseudo-participation
Manipulation	

But while such typologies and hierarchies of participation may be helpful in revealing some of the multiple meanings of the term, in doing so they also invite us to question whether the term has any real meaning at all. Is it helpful to have a term whose meanings stretch all the way from manipulated consultation to liberation from oppression? Alfonso Gumucio-Dagron (2001: 8) does see real value in the looseness of the term, arguing that 'the eagerness for labels and encapsulated definitions could only contribute to freeze a communication movement that is still shaping itself, and that may be more valuable precisely because of its variety and looseness'. However, Robert Huesca (2002: 209) sees this lack of clarity in more sinister terms, arguing that 'the concept of participatory communication is subject to loose interpretation that appears at best to be variable and at worst misused and distorted'. Indeed, does preserving the ambiguity of this term not serve primarily to maintain its rhetorical value? As long as the precise meaning of the term participation remains unclear, its association with ideas like equality and self-determination will be used to mask the adoption of practices that are, in reality, towards the lower end of Arnstein's ladder. It is commonly observed that the term has been used to legitimize the continuation of practices associated with the M4D approach. As Paulo Escobar (1999: 326) has argued, the call for participation in the 1970s was 'easily co-opted by the established system and rendered ineffective or counterproductive'. It is on this basis that participation has been accused of becoming 'the new tyranny' (Cooke and Kothari 2001) in development and of being a 'double agent of deception' (Sonderling 1997) because of its redeeming effect on 'top-down', modernization practices. If this is indeed the case, what is to be done? Would a more sophisticated or nuanced vocabulary help? Does drawing attention to this practice help to ameliorate it? Is a radical interpretation of participatory communication now no longer even possible?

Whatever the answers to these questions, it should be clear

that while drawing a distinction between diffusion and participation models of communication is useful for providing a clear
overview of participatory communication, it also provokes more
critical questions about its coherence and relevance.

New technologies and participatory communication

Notably absent from the discussion so far has been mention of
the role of new information and communication technologies
in participatory communication. Examples abound of the apparent transformative potential for social and mobile media in
particular; for protest movements (in North Africa in 2011, for
example), humanitarian responses (in Haiti, 2010, and Japan,
2011, for example) and elections (in Senegal, 2012, and Kenya,
2013). Associated claims that new media provide 'greater opportunities for engagement and participation of individuals and
communities' (Obregon 2012: 69) are now commonplace. The
premise of such assertions is that there is something distinctive about the inherent properties of new technologies, which
lend themselves to facilitating participatory communication.
But what might these peculiarities be?

**The affordances of new technologies: promoting participa-
tion** Manuel Castells is perhaps the most famous academic
in this area and his work provides a useful starting point for
helping us to answer this question. In *The Rise of the Network Society* (2010: xviii) his central thesis is that a new global
social structure is being created, which he refers to as 'the
network society' because 'it is made of networks in all the key
dimensions of social organisation and social practice'. Castells
(ibid.: xxx) argues that this transformation is being driven by

new digital technologies which have helped to overcome the traditional limitations of networking organizations and which have instead 'powered social and organisational networks in ways that allowed their endless expansion and reconfiguration'. Castells (2007: 246) uses the phrase 'mass self-communication' to describe the rise of a new form of mass, multi-modal, socialized, self-generated, self-directed and self-selected communication, which new technologies have permitted: 'The communication foundation of the network society is the global web of horizontal communication networks that include the multimodal exchange of interactive messages from many to many both synchronous and asynchronous.'

There are obvious similarities between the interactive, horizontal networks of communication characteristic of mass self-communication and the characteristics of participatory communication in development discussed above. Castells himself (ibid.: 248) goes on to consider explicitly how mass self-communication has enabled new forms of 'counter-power', or the capacity by social actors to challenge and eventually change the power relations institutionalized in society. He writes that

> The greater the autonomy provided to the users by the
> technologies of communication, the greater the chances that
> new values and new interests will enter the realm of socialised
> communication, so reaching the public mind. Thus, the rise
> of mass self-communication … enhances the opportunities
> for social change, without however defining the content and
> purpose of such social change. (Castells 2009: 8)

In his influential book *Here Comes Everybody*, Clay Shirky (2009) explains how new technologies have made group inter-action and group action, outside the framework of traditional institutions and organizations, 'ridiculously easy'. Specifically, he argues that new technologies have caused a collapse in the costs (i.e. time, effort and attention) of creating a new group or joining an existing one. This fact, combined with what he describes as our 'native talent' for group action, has led to

> A remarkable increase in our ability to share, to cooperate with one another, and to take collective action ... By making it easier for groups to self-assemble and for individuals to contribute to group effort without requiring formal management, these tools have radically altered the old limits on the size, sophistication, and scope of unsupervised effort. (Ibid.: 21)

Shirky also applies his broad account of the affordances of new technologies more specifically to the context of participatory communication in social change. In 'The political power of social media' (2011), he offers an 'environmental' view of social media as a long-term tool for strengthening civil society and the public sphere. Shirky (ibid.: 5) argues that by spreading, not just media consumption, but media production as well, 'it allows people to privately and publicly articulate and debate a welter of conflicting views'. Put another way, the internet provides not just greater access to information, compared to other media, but also far greater 'access to conversation'. Shirky applies this idea to Katz and Lazarsfeld's 'two step flow' model of communication (see Chapter 1) to suggest that whereas mass media may be crucial to the first 'step', social media amplify the second.

Moreover, Shirky outlines how social media have a particular tendency to promote anti-hierarchical forms of group coordination within political movements. The way social media enable messages to be spread rapidly though social networks, he argues, creates a 'shared awareness' of a situation. This shared awareness can not only mobilize political movements quickly but also horizontally – in the form of 'loosely coordinated publics' which don't rely on conventional, institutional, hierarchies.

From this brief account of the work of just two authors, we

can identify a number of characteristics of new technologies which may indeed suggest a tendency to encourage participatory communication. These include a propensity to promote interactivity and debate, to facilitate decentralized, 'flat', networks which do not rely on institutional structures, as well as a tendency to promote greater individual autonomy in communication. This is certainly not an exhaustive list. According to Philip Howard and Muzammil Hussain (2013: 3), digital media had a causal role in the Arab Spring because, among other things, they 'allowed communities to realise that they shared grievances and because they nurtured transportable strategies for mobilizing against dictators'. We might also ask to what extent new technologies liberate us from concentrations of ownership, allowing new forms of community ownership and control? They also appear to offer us the ability to communicate much more freely across national and cultural boundaries.

The affordances of new technologies: suppressing participation In reflecting critically on these ideas, we might ask whether focusing only on the *potential* of new technologies to *promote* participatory communication amounts to 'cyber-utopianism'. Evgeny Morozov (2011: xii) defines this as 'a naïve belief in the emancipatory nature of online communication that rests on a stubborn refusal to acknowledge its downside'. Indeed, it is equally possible to identify a number of other apparent properties of new technologies which appear to work against their suitability for participatory communication.

Primarily, the nature of new technologies and the resources and capabilities required to make use of them can mean that it is only those who are 'technologically privileged' (Fenton and Barassi 2011: 179) who can take part in the forms of communication which they permit. In 2013, an estimated 39 per cent of the world's population had access to the internet (ITU 2013).

While such statistics are often interpreted as evidence that the internet has been 'brought to nearly every corner of the globe' (Kaplan 2012: 34), they can equally be seen as further evidence of the persistence of stark inequalities in access. Although 75 per cent of people in Europe may be online, the same is true for just 16 per cent of people in Africa (ITU 2013). A grossly uneven distribution of access is even more apparent within societies. Technologies of 'mass self-communication' are generally more expensive to buy and maintain (and they can also become obsolete relatively very quickly and need replacing). They also require users to have the time and sufficient (media) literacy (see Chapter 3) to use them. Even if users are able to get online, they may struggle to find locally relevant content in an appropriate language. The inevitable consequence is that it is the most marginalized who are excluded from access. This is clearly not conducive to participatory communication. To be clear, though, it does not follow that providing greater access to new technologies, or 'bridging the digital divide', is necessarily the solution. Uneven access to the internet is a symptom of wider social, political and economic inequalities and the provision of new technologies alone will not solve this.

Secondly, while new technologies may, given the right conditions, help to facilitate participatory communication, they also afford repressive governments new opportunities to monitor public and private communications and to suppress dissent (Morozov 2011; MacKinnon 2012). As David Kaplan (2012: 36) argues, 'Digital surveillance is far cheaper and faster than the old "analog" techniques of wiretapping and bugging one's home and office. Breaking into the account of just one activist or journalist could quickly lead to entire networks of friends and associates, compromising the security of dozens of people.'

In 2011 the internet was censored in more than forty different countries, affecting over a half-billion users (ibid.: 36). Revelations about the extent of the US National Security Agency's (NSA) surveillance programme in 2013 illustrate how everyday online activities generate vast amounts of data which can be monitored by governments. Under such conditions, to what extent can new technologies genuinely provide the kinds of spaces necessary for participatory communication?

Thirdly, Malcolm Gladwell (2010) has famously argued that the kinds of ties between individuals within a network that are sustained by social media are much weaker than the ties between individuals offline, who communicate and interact face to face. This matters, Gladwell suggests, because it affects the resulting forms of collective action which such groups can engage in. Whereas strong ties are required for high-risk (offline) activism that explicitly confronts socially entrenched norms and practices, the weak ties sustained by social media produce little more than 'clicktivism'. Gladwell (ibid.) explains that 'Facebook activism succeeds not by motivating people to make a real sacrifice but by motivating them to do the things that people do when they are not motivated enough to make a real sacrifice'. Social media may increase levels of participation, but only because participation is made easier, not because people are more motivated to take part. In his response to this argument, Shirky (2011: 7) points out that while 'clicktivism' may exist, it doesn't mean that those individuals who are committed cannot also use social media to coordinate real-world action.

Fourthly, while the political mobilizations in North Africa and the Middle East in 2011 may have demonstrated that new technologies can certainly enable groups to coordinate responses to events rapidly and en masse, events thereafter have suggested that such technologies may be less suitable to long-term political organization and mobilization. In Shirky's (2009) terminology, we might argue that while social media may lower the 'costs of co-ordination' of social movements and enable group mobilization based on 'ad hoc synchronisation', they also produce 'undisciplined' or loosely organized groups which lack the means of sustaining political mobilizations in the longer term. In an explicit critique of Shirky's work, Gladwell (2010) argues that a centralized leadership structure and clear lines of authority are necessary for thinking and acting strategically, and that such strategic thinking is necessary for effecting systematic change over the long term.

> How do you make difficult choices about tactics or strategy or philosophical direction when everyone has an equal say? ... If you're taking on a powerful and organized establishment you have to be a hierarchy ... The instruments of social media ... make it easier for activists to express themselves, and harder for that expression to have any impact.

Fifthly, Natalie Fenton and Veronica Barassi (2011) argue that although the individualistic logic of social media may promote self-expression among individuals, which may contribute to participatory communication and political action in the way that Castells suggests, this logic can also work *against* collective forms of participation. Specifically, they suggest that by enabling individual creative autonomy, social media may, among other things, inhibit the construction of a collective voice and of a collective symbolic identity within political groups; both of which are central to the development of collective action (ibid.: 188). As the director of the NGO they were researching commented, 'what should we do when the message of a single 11-year-old can achieve a greater importance than our own?' Fenton and Barassi (ibid.: 193) conclude by asking, 'do social media do no more than serve ego-centred needs and reflect practices structured around the self even in the nonmainstream world of alternative media? These practices may be liberating for the user but not necessarily democratizing for society.'

Finally, there is an argument which suggests that rather than encouraging diverse groups to communicate with each other, new technologies might actually encourage self-segregation and polarization (Lawrence et al. 2009). The claim is that since new technologies provide us with more control over what we consume and whom we interact with, we are increasingly able to satisfy our tendency to prefer more comfortable, self-affirming interactions with those already in our 'in-groups', rather than those who might challenge our existing views. One of the consequences of this, Cass Sunstein (2008) suggests, is that increased deliberation among like-minded people is likely to promote both more extreme views and greater consensus within those groups (or a lack of diversity). By contrast, although 'old' media may offer audiences less choice over whom to interact with, by confronting us (collectively) with people and experiences which we might not otherwise seek out, they may (inadvertently) promote a greater degree of mutual respect and collective deliberation.

Do the affordances of new technologies really matter? Having discussed some of the possible features of new technologies which may both lend themselves to, and detract from, the ability to promote participatory communication, what conclusion should we reach? Is it enough to recognize that new technologies potentially have both 'positive' and 'negative' effects? Or does such a conclusion not blind us to more productive questions? At the very least, this discussion should have encouraged us to be sceptical of sweeping claims about how new technologies inevitably promote participatory communication in all contexts. In which case, should we not be asking what drives techno-optimist accounts of new technologies? Whose interests do they serve?

We might also wish to consider to what extent we may be guilty of technological determinism – of assuming that the nature of the technology alone will drive change. Morozov (2011: xvi) refers to this perspective as 'internet-centrism', or a belief that it will shape every environment that it penetrates, rather than vice versa. Even Castells (2010: xxxi) recognizes that 'the medium, even a medium as revolutionary as [the internet], does not determine the content and effect of its messages'. Such internet-centrism treats the internet as a constant and diverts attention away from 'the many forces that are shaping the internet – not all of them for the better' (Morozov 2011: xvi). Don Slater (2013: 18) refers to this as 'media essentialism', or the idea that (new) media have intrinsic properties, independent of their social contexts, that are fixed and universal (rather than emergent and relational) and whose 'impact' can be observed and measured in any given location. He even goes so far as to suggest replacing terms like 'media' and 'new media', which are associated with a particular Northern view of the world, with the emptier notions of 'communicative assemblages' and 'communicative ecology'.

One response to accusations of internet-centrism and media essentialism is to focus, not on the affordances or impacts of new technologies, but on what each individual context requires and whether and how technology can play a role in this (Morozov 2011; Gumucio-Dagron 2003). Another is, as Rebecca MacKinnon (2012: xx) suggests, to 'stop debating *whether* the Internet is an effective tool for political expression, and to move on to the much more urgent question of how digital technology can be structured, governed and used to maximise the good it can do in the world, and minimise the evil'. Ultimately, readers must consider for themselves how the arguments discussed above should be reconciled – based, at least partly, on whether they challenge or confirm their own personal experiences involving new technologies and participatory communication.

Conclusion

This chapter leaves open the question of what role, if any, media play in (different forms of) participatory communication. Some basic points have been made about the primacy of interpersonal communication and the importance of indigenous communications systems. Beyond this, though, this chapter should be taken only as a starting point for considering in more detail what the affordances of different media might be and how important these are, or are not, in different contexts – or whether technologies have fixed properties at all. All the while, we must recognize that convergence, or the interaction between different media, makes the answers to these questions even more complex.

Another dimension of participatory communication which readers may want to reflect further upon is the implications for the role of the facilitator. Broadly speaking, their role is to act as a catalyst in the empowerment of others who are different from themselves, without controlling the process and while maintaining a genuine respect for local knowledge. This is not easy, particularly because of the 'marks of their origin' (Freire 1970: 42) they inevitabley bring with them. As Servaes (1996: 24) has argued, aside from class and organizational interests, the attitude of the facilitator – and 'large egos and self-righteousness' in particular – is perhaps the major obstacle to participation. In this context, I find the following passage particularly challenging.

> Participatory communication requires first of all changes in the thinking of 'communicators'. The needles and targets of development communication models, combined with self-righteousness, titles, and misdirected benevolence, often render 'experts' a bit too pompous and pushy. Perhaps this is because it requires much more imagination, preparation and hard work

to have dialogical learning. It is far easier to prepare and give lectures. (Servaes and Malikhao 2005: 91)

Finally, readers may wish to consider whether there are limits to participation and, if so, what these limits might be. Does everyone always need to be involved in all aspects of development? Might this not lead to either the 'banalization' of participation or to gross inefficiencies in the process (Bordenave 1994: 46)? Since participation takes precious time away from other activities, should we not recognize that there might be occasions on which participating is simply not worth it?

3 | Defining Media Development: Nailing Jelly to a Wall

According to the results of survey data from Freedom House (2013) there has been no overall progress in levels of press freedom in the world in general since the significant advances in media freedoms in central and eastern Europe in the early 1990s. In fact, between 2002 and 2012 levels of press freedom in the world in general actually declined year on year, with the exception of a minor overall improvement in 2011 as a result of the 'Arab Spring'. While Tunisia and Libya largely retained gains in media freedom in 2012, Egypt experienced significant backsliding and the percentage of the world's population living in societies with a fully free press fell to its lowest level in over a decade. In 2012, fewer than 14 per cent of the world's inhabitants lived in countries with a free press, while 43 per cent experienced a partly free press and another 43 per cent lived in not-free environments (ibid.).

Such concerns for levels of media freedom are central to the field known as media development. The aim of this chapter is to provide an all-too-rare critical account of the multiple, contested and often rather confusing ways in which media development is defined, measured and practised. In pursuit of this aim, this chapter addresses the following questions: what is media development – or what do developed media look like (media development as an outcome) – and what activities might we pursue in order to help achieve this (media development as a set of activities)? The question 'why develop the media?' is dealt with in Chapter 4.

This chapter begins by reviewing the role of seven key factors at the heart of understandings of media development – independence, plurality, professionalism, capacity, an enabling environment, economic sustainability and media literacy. In order to offer a rich and comprehensive account of media development, particular emphasis is intentionally given to those dimensions of the concept which are often overlooked – especially media literacy. The second half of this chapter then outlines four further debates in defining media development: the distinction between media development and media for development (M4D), the importance of external actors, the role of different technologies and the relevance of universal indicators used to measure media development. Indeed, this chapter has already entered into one of these controversies by opening with a discussion of Freedom House's data in a way that presents media development as a universal norm that can be applied and measured equally in any given country. The chapter will reveal how this seemingly innocuous opening can be considered deeply problematic.

This is certainly not just an academic exercise. How we understand media development has consequences for the conduct, evaluation, outcome and priority given to media development interventions. As Kathy Lines (2009: 6, 16) explains,

> Defining media [development] ... impacts on how it is dealt with at all levels – from policy level to programmatic support ... Without a generally accepted definition, it is hard to monitor precisely what is being done in the field, and thereby to easily measure progress in terms of spend, programmes or research ... And without such a definition, there may continue to be a gap between what is said and what is done.

Defining media development

Media development as freedom At the heart of all understandings of media development is a concern for media freedom. This focus on freedom stems, primarily, from a liberal approach to the function of the media in a democracy in which the media are understood to be unable to perform their role as a public watchdog – overseeing the actions of the state – if they are in fact subject to the influence of the state. A World Bank (2002: 183) study of the ownership of the largest newspapers, television stations and radio stations in ninety-seven different countries found that 'on average, the state controls about 30 percent of the top five newspapers and 60 percent of the top five television stations in these countries. The state also owns a huge share – 72 percent – of the largest radio stations.' Such patterns of ownership suggest that the media are unlikely to be able to expose abuses of power by the state in many cases.

In this context, the argument is often made that the media should instead be in private hands, anchored to the free market, to ensure a significant degree of independence from the government. However, being linked to private/corporate interests, rather than state interests, may merely shift the problem of independence rather than resolve it, particularly if ownership is concentrated in the hands of a small number of powerful individuals (Curran 2000: 84). Indeed, the results of the aforementioned World Bank (2002) study found that the vast majority of large newspapers and television and radio stations not controlled by the state were in fact owned by families (often with close links to the state), rather than in widely dispersed shareholdings. James Curran (2000: 86) argues that the trend towards privatization has resulted in the media increasingly being embedded in the corporate structure of big business. One of the consequences of this pattern of ownership, he suggests, is that the media are more likely to refrain from criticizing or investigating the actions of the giant conglomerates to which they belong, or the broader system of global capitalism upon which they depend. As was argued in the *China Daily* in December 2011, 'isn't it surprising the almighty media in the U.S. didn't get wind of the global financial crisis, created by greedy tycoons and their executives, let alone suggest precautionary measures?' (cited in Nelson and Susman-Peña 2012).

In brief, a concern for media freedom refers to freedom not only from undue political influence from the state or other political interests (as in classic liberal theory), but also from private and corporate interests and from vested interests more generally.

Press plurality If we accept that, in spite of efforts to remain as free as possible from the influence of vested interests, all media organizations will inevitably have their own agendas and priorities, then press plurality becomes a second vital aspect of media development. The basic idea is that plurality prevents one media owner or outlet from having too much influence by ensuring that the public sphere is populated by multiple voices and perspectives.

Plurality refers, not only to the *number* of media outlets, but to the diversity in *content* and *ownership* of those outlets. In the UNESCO *Declaration of Windhoek* (1991), for example, a pluralistic press is defined as 'the end of monopolies of any kind and the existence of the greatest possible number of newspapers, magazines and periodicals reflecting the widest possible range of opinion within the community'. This distinction between quantity and diversity is important because, as Mark Wilson and Kitty Warnock (2007) argue, despite a growth in the overall number of media outlets in most countries in the global South in the 1980s and 1990s, this masked the continuation of an extremely narrow range of voices and views. This is because unregulated growth can bring concentrations of ownership, whereby only a small number of individuals or organizations can afford the high entry costs associated with media ownership. Katharine Allen and Iginio Gagliardone (2011) point out that in Kenya, although there are more than 7 daily newspapers, 100 radio stations, 17 television stations and 13 weekly and monthly papers, the market is dominated by four groups – the Nation Media Group, the Standard Media Group, the Royal Media Group and Radio Africa. Allen and Gagliardone (ibid.: 13) argue that the major media houses are reinforcing barriers to market entry in the media sector by 'using methods ranging from interference with licensing procedures to monopolizing advertising and distribution networks'.

One way of attempting to prevent such concentrations of ownership and of prompting plurality is by passing and enforcing specific regulations limiting the influence which a single person, family, company or group may have in one or more media sectors. According to the UNESCO framework for assessing media development (2008: 3), such rules can include thresholds on audience share or turnover/revenue and should take into account both horizontal integration (mergers within the same branch of activity) and vertical integration (control by a single person, company or group of key elements of the production and distribution processes).

Plurality can also be promoted more directly by funding media outlets, as is now often the case in fragile states or countries experiencing democratic transition. However, Tim Allen and Nicole Stremlau (2005: 219) warn against simply promoting plurality for its own sake.

Some agencies, such as USAID, have been known to subsidize anti-government papers that are barely comprehensible for the sole reason they are anti-government or have encouraged ethnic-related media outlets to proliferate. These policies are made with the idea that they will contribute to a variety of perspectives and thus promote understanding and peace.

While it is easy to see why media plurality is important, there are limits to how wide ranging public discourse should be allowed to be. For instances of hate speech, or more generally where freedom of speech conflicts with other values or rights, there is a case for introducing some limits. In the UK, for example, the law forbids any communication that is threatening, abusive or insulting, or which is intended to harass, alarm or distress. Communications that involve obscenity, child pornography, defamation, slander or which are owned by others may also require restrictions. The question of where these limits should be set – and of when striking a balance between different rights and values becomes an excuse for state censorship – is a matter of judgement for every society. The overall point remains, though, that another cornerstone of media development is the promotion of media plurality, or of the greatest possible number and range of media outlets, within reason.

Professionalism, capacity and an enabling environment Another key dimension of media development is the efforts aimed at capacity-building/strengthening of the media sector. Although this can include a wide range of activities designed to support media organizations, the most common and indeed the most well-funded area of media development overall is journalist training. An estimated 50 per cent of USAID's media development funding is targeted here, although this has declined from an estimated 80 or 90 per cent of such funding in the 1990s (Mottaz 2010). Such training can be delivered 'on the job' through employers or as part of structured courses and qualification programmes in universities, journalism schools or through international institutions. Topics covered range from media ethics and the basic skills of fact-gathering and writing, to the techniques of investigative reporting and election coverage. Such journalistic training forms part of a wider umbrella of activities designed to support media professionalism in general, including support for trade unions and other professional associations.

Aside from suitable training, those working in the media also require appropriate infrastructural and technical support if they are to perform their roles fully. This can include the provision of digital media technology, production equipment and satellite technology to allow for efficient news gathering, production and distribution (UNESCO 2008). In fact, it appears that the traditional focus on journalism training is at least partly being replaced by an increasing focus on ICT provision. Support for ICT grew from virtually 0 per cent to 17 per cent of media development assistance between 2002 and 2008 (Kaufman 2012). Laura Mottaz (2010: 39) reports that 'today nearly every U.S. media development grant encourages – and often requires – the incorporation of digital components'.

Capacity-building/strengthening within the media sector is clearly important if the media are to be free to engage effectively in producing content and disseminating information and ideas. But while such training and infrastructure support may be useful in countries with legal frameworks and political environments that protect freedom of expression, if this legal framework and a broader culture supportive of press freedom is not in place, then the outcomes of capacity-building initiatives are likely to be limited. As Kennedy Javuru (2012: 1) puts it, 'if the system isn't free, a well trained journalist won't make it so'. In this context, Tara Susman-Peña (2012: 54) argues that

Despite years of policy papers decrying the ineffectiveness of short-term trainings, they are still being funded on a large scale. Even long-term training by itself does not professionalize the media sector, because of a host of contextual factors at play … Trainings without a focus on the broader enabling environment may improve the practice of some individuals, but do not professionalize the sector. Africa needs support for its journalism schools, and long-term training, together with improvements in the enabling environment.

This enabling environment consists, to some degree, of a legal and regulatory framework supporting media independence. The legal tools which can be used to either suppress or promote media independence can be divided into three main areas: news gathering (including freedom of information laws, protection of confidential sources and the licensing of journalists), content-based regulation (including criminal defamation, libel, privacy and 'insult' laws as well as national security statutes) and protection of journalists in their professional activity (including a willingness by authorities to prosecute those who physically intimidate or attack media representatives) (Krug and Price 2002). Repressive laws often don't even have to be regularly enacted to have an impact on the press as the 'chilling effect' of a small number of cases can lead to self-censorship.

One notable area in which significant progress has been made in recent years regarding an enabling legal environment is in the passing of freedom of information laws. As of January 2012, at least ninety countries had nationwide laws establishing the right of, and procedures for, the public to request and receive government-held information (Right2info 2012). This included more than half of the countries in Latin America, more than a dozen in Asia and the Pacific, ten countries in Africa, and two in the Middle East. Most of these laws have been passed in the last decade (Kaplan 2012: 60). 'As of May 2012, when Brazil's law entered into force, some 5.5 billion people live in countries that include in their domestic law an enforceable right, at least in theory, to obtain information from their governments' (Right2info 2012).

Such laws can provide journalists with an important tool for exposing government corruption. In India, for example, the 2005 Right to Information Act has had a significant effect on the media's ability to make public persons and institutions accountable. There are now annual Right to Information (RTI) awards. In 2010, for example, the RTI Journalist Award went to Saikat Dutta of *Outlook*, who used the Right to Information Act to expose a rice export scam in India worth over US$400 million.

But despite progress in this particular area, and despite an enabling legal environment being a key structural determinant of a free press, broader improvements have proved exceptionally difficult to achieve. The necessary costs, time and unpredictability of such efforts, as well as the need to engage with multiple stakeholders (not just the media) and often to directly challenge existing power relations, all provide disincentives for donors to work in this area. Local actors are usually much better placed than donors to offer the sustained commitment required for systemic change. In 2011, only 5 per cent of US media development assistance was estimated to have been directed at supporting a legal enabling environment (Kaplan 2012: 17).

Furthermore, even if suitable laws are formally adopted, unless there is support from the institutions charged with implementing these laws, there is no guarantee that they will be effective. While an increasing number of countries may have freedom of information laws, for example, they are often poorly implemented. In 2010, a network of freedom of information advocacy groups in Indonesia conducted an 'access test' of the country's newly implemented law and found that 70 per cent of the 347 requests they made were either denied or ignored (Basorie 2011). As Krug and Price (2002: 188) put it, 'the whole concept of an enabling environment implies that specific laws exist in a context in which the spirit of the laws is engaged and the processes for realizing their impact are implemented'.

A crucial part of this context is the informal codes of conduct within the media industry and the more general culture and expectations within society. For example, although the United Kingdom has had a rather restrictive Official Secrets Act, the media have had a long tradition of independence and the British media rank highly on any measure of freedom (Islam 2002a). Conversely, in countries where freedom of information has a less well-established history, a culture of secrecy can severely dilute the effectiveness of any new legislation, as was the case in Indonesia. Roumeen Islam (ibid.) suggests that the potential value of more information can be underestimated or not well understood, and that the public often perceives that information alone will not help (because coalitions strong enough to make use of the available information do not exist).

It is in this context that one of three key conclusions of a recent report on the state of international media development arose:

> The international development community needs to spend
> less time training journalists and more time on efforts to build
> country level leadership for a strong and independent media as
> a key institution of development. This means longer-term pro-
> grams, facilitating carefully planned and rigorous approaches
> to multi-stakeholder engagement, and South–South knowledge
> exchange led by local champions. (Nelson and Susman-Peña
> 2012: 5)

In summary, professional and technical capacity matter, but only to the extent that an enabling environment allows.

Economic sustainability The importance of the economic viability of media organizations in media development is a surprisingly contested issue. On the one hand, it is apparent that if media outlets are economically self-sustaining then they will be better able to remain free from political and economic interests. Poorly paid journalists are more likely to accept money in exchange for favourable coverage than well-paid journalists, no matter how well trained they are. The chief editor of a large newspaper in Kinshasa explains this in the following way:

> How can I refuse to sign and publish a piece drafted and brought to me by a political party when publishing that piece can bring me $300, at the exact moment when my landlord threatens to throw me out and when my children have been expelled from school for not having paid school fees? (cited in Frère 2011: 18)

In light of this, training in business skills and in the collection and use of market and audience data to make media outlets commercially viable is now accepted as an important dimension of media development.

Yet the requirement of economic sustainability brings other problems. Advertising is often controlled by the government and a small number of large companies, which can use this as a mechanism for exerting influence. Equally, the need to attract and retain audiences in a competitive market is not necessarily conducive to the production of high-quality, diverse and informative content. For example, while the number of private news channels in India may have increased dramatically in recent years, these channels have been criticized for resorting to 'infotainment' (Thussu 2007) and catering only to the urban middle classes (Batabyal 2012). 'News bulletins rarely, if ever, carry detailed reports on education or health, rather ... the focus is on the three Cs – crime, cricket and cinema ... In a market-driven media environment, such populism ... may in fact be undermining the quality of public debate (Thussu 2007: 607–8).

In this context, dependence on donor support can be seen as acceptable if media outlets are serving an important role in society. If a community radio station is providing local people with information and with a voice that would not otherwise be available, does it really matter if it relies to some extent upon donor support? Radio Miraya in South Sudan, for example, is part of a UN radio project that costs $5 million annually (Myers 2012a: 18) but it provides a vital source of news in a region with few alternative sources of information. Indeed, public service broadcasting in many Western countries requires continuous state, or non-commercial, support, yet is widely regarded as an important part of a plural media system.

But this approach is also problematic, since donor dependence is hardly conducive to truly free media. Donors are frequently criticized for funding economically unsustainable media outlets, to promote a particular agenda, for a short time, which then collapse when their support ends. Jorgen Ejboel (2006: 66) describes a form of 'donor sickness' in Central Asia, whereby 'many newspapers there have been given money for many years and now find it very difficult to work on their own without financial help. Financial aid has become a drug for both them and the donors, who make a great living handing out money.' Disproportionate financial support from donors has also been accused of distorting the local market, luring skilled workers away from local media outlets by offering higher salaries and creating expectations among audiences for a level of professionalism which cannot be achieved once they have gone (Susman-Peña 2012). In summary, while it is clear that economic considerations are fundamental to media development, there are no obvious answers to the question of where the money should come from.

Media literacy Independent and plural media depend, not only on the professionalism and sustainability of the work of media professionals, but also on the involvement of citizens. A free press is not free if the public cannot access it, understand it and contribute to the creation of it. Thus, a further dimension of media development must be the media literacy of the citizenry.

The concept of media literacy first became popular as a means of talking about the ability of citizens (and particularly children) to protect themselves from the perceived harms of the media. In this understanding, emphasis is placed upon citizens' ability to understand (and critique) communications, or 'the ability to understand that all media content is "constructed" ... [and] has embedded values and points of view' (Kellner and Share 2005: 376). In the context of media development, this refers to citizens' ability to act as critical consumers of propaganda or hate speech. In Rwanda, for example, the Great Lakes Reconciliation Radio Project uses a combination of formal media literacy education, public debate programmes and listening groups to encourage audiences to think critically about media content and sensitize them to potential media manipulation. In this way, media literacy education may be understood as a more effective alternative to state control of media content; shifting responsibility to the receiving end of communications, rather than the production end (Moeller 2009).

More recently the concept of media literacy has been associated, not only with an ability to protect oneself from the perceived harms of the media, but with the skills necessary to create media or use them to communicate. In fact, this understanding of media literacy is at the heart of the Media Mapping Project's (see Arsenault and Powers 2010: 7) definition of media development as 'the process of improving the media's ability to communicate with the public, and the process of improving the public's ability to communicate, using media'.

This ability to create media is seen as increasingly fundamental to democratic participation and empowerment in modern information societies. It is necessary for the functioning of community media, which, in most contexts, rely almost entirely on citizens who are not professional journalists. It also makes possible citizen journalism, which has become a vital tool for documenting government abuses and enabling citizens to take part in mainstream media discourse.

More fundamentally, a media-literate citizenry must also have the ability to physically access the media and to use them. From the point of view of governance, the issue of access matters in at least two ways (Norris and Odugbemi 2010b). First, nation-building and state effectiveness rely on the capacity of the government to be able to communicate with all citizens. Secondly, access to the media is of fundamental importance to citizenship. The public requires access to multiple sources of information if they are to make informed choices during elections, for example.

Finally, understandings of media literacy in the context of development often emphasize the need for citizens (and elites) to have a critical appreciation of the role of the media in society. This, it is argued, creates an expectation and a demand among the public for a free and independent press, which can contribute to its achievement. Such support can be seen implicitly in the daily decisions of many audiences living under repressive regimes to seek out and consume alternative sources of information online, where possible, but also more overtly when citizens take action to protect the freedom of the press. For example, in March 2006 Kenyan security forces raided the offices of the newspaper *The Standard*, which had been reporting on possible corrupt behaviour by officials in government. In response, thousands of citizens mobilized in support of the newspaper. This led to a parliamentary hearing and the government's cessation of its alleged intimidation (Tettey 2010). If the public were not sufficiently supportive of the principle of press freedom this would likely not have happened.

In summary, media literacy can be defined as the ability of citizens to access, understand and create communications and to understand the functions of the media and their rights in relation to it (see Ofcom 2006). Arguments about the importance of media literacy education have been made strongly in several western European countries in debates about educational curricula. In the UK, for example, in 2004, the then minister for media, culture and sport, Tessa Jowell, remarked that, 'I believe that in the modern world, media literacy will become as important a skill as maths or science'. Despite this, in the development sector, the concept of media literacy remains widely unrecognized. In 2011 it accounted for only an estimated 4 per cent of US media development funding (although this did represent an increase from 0.2 per cent in 2006) (Kaplan 2012).

Media literacy interventions face many challenges, including the length of time taken to produce results and difficulties in isolating and quantifying their impact (Moeller 2009). Furthermore, while the concept of media literacy may be useful for drawing attention to the variety of important ways in which citizens' media-related competencies matter, the many different interpretations of the term call into question the value of such an 'expansive and unstable' (Hobbs 1998: 16) concept. Put another way, media literacy is a concept which can be used to explain everything in general about citizens' uses of media and hence nothing in particular. As a result, it can be presented, perhaps rather unhelpfully, as a magic bullet for achieving a wide range of development objectives. In the Alexandria Proclamation of 2005, for example, the related concepts of information literacy and lifelong learning are described as

Beacons of the Information Society, illuminating the courses to development, prosperity and freedom. Information literacy empowers people in all walks of life to seek, evaluate, use and create information effectively to achieve their personal, social, occupational and educational goals. It is a basic human right in a digital world and promotes social inclusion in all nations.

A final issue is that in seeking to promote media literacy, there is a danger of advocating a *universal* set of competencies that are applicable in all contexts. As Sandy Campbell (2004: 2) explains, when we think of a media or information-literature user,

> We think of people who can use a computer, connect to the internet, access a variety of kinds of information, distinguish between levels of quality and validity of information, comprehend the content of the information so that they can apply it and are aware of the rules around the use of information.

Yet this is a decidedly narrow definition, which fails to take into account local conditions (Dunn and Johnson-Brown 2008). To be a competent and critical user of media in Papua New Guinea, Chad or Mongolia, for example, is likely to mean something very different to what it does in France or the USA. As Douglas Kellner and Jeff Share (2005: 369) argue, 'literacies are socially constructed ... [and] evolve and shift in response to social and cultural change and the interests of elites who control hegemonic institutions'.

In a related critique, Fackson Banda (2009: 225) describes media education in Africa as being characterized by 'the liberal journalistic epistemic orientation which privileges dispassionate media work over civically active media practice'. According to Banda, the emphasis in Western approaches to media education is on technical skills, as opposed to critical engagement, which favours 'the speedy production of graduates to staff profit-seeking media conglomerates' rather than a critical analysis of the relevance of Western professional norms and practices in African contexts. He goes on to advocate for a post-colonial educational agenda in African journalism training which reflects 'the specificity of African cultures and invoke[s] the moral agency of African journalists'. Specifically, Banda points to how the African ethic of 'ubuntu' leads to a reconceptualization of journalistic autonomy.

In light of such critiques of a universalist perspective on media literacy, Hopeton Dunn and Sheena Johnson-Brown (2008) suggest we focus on the existence of multiple media *literacies*, which are determined by the cultural, political and historical contexts of the community in which they are used. If we accept this point, then a compelling case can be made for drawing attention to the importance of media literacies in both constituting and enabling a free and independent media sector.

In summary, it should be clear that there is no single most important pillar of media development. Developed media and the effective promotion of them require the coexistence of a number of mutually dependent factors, including independence, pluralism, professionalism, capacity, an enabling environment, economic sustainability and a media-literate public. While the politics of aid may mean that some of these factors, such as plurality and professionalism, may be easier to support and receive greater attention, I have argued here that other factors, including media literacy and an enabling environment, are equally important. But listing the key features of media development is only one way of getting to grips with the multiple meanings and interpretations of this slippery concept. As we move into discussing four further debates in this field, we will see that contestation over the meaning of the term media development is vigorous and highly political.

Defining media development through media for development

A common way of defining and understanding the field of media development is in opposition to media for development (M4D). M4D is concerned with using the media as a tool or instrument in pursuit of specific development objectives, such as modified health behaviours (as discussed in Chapter 1). By contrast, the target of media development is the development of media themselves. The media are viewed as being important in their own right, and not simply as a tool for delivering messages that persuade audiences to wear condoms or boil water, for example. In this approach, it is the media industry which requires support, or media *development*.

Yet this distinction between media development and M4D is not as obvious as it might first appear. Just as M4D seeks to achieve specific development outcomes, so discourses on media development also have a strong normative dimension. Most proponents of media development advocate, not for a general expansion of the media in any given way, but for a certain kind of media playing a certain kind of function in society – most notably, one that is linked to democracy and good governance (see Chapter 4). As James Dean (2008: 1) asks (of himself in a rhetorical conversation):

> Aren't you talking about a certain type of media – a media
> that serves the public good, which holds governments to
> account, which is plural and acts in the interest of all citizens?
> Aren't you actually talking about media that serves a set of
> social objectives which development organisations share? You
> aren't talking about a media that just serves a political or eco-
> nomic elite ... So in effect you are talking about media in the
> context of a certain kind of development outcome.

Put another way, in media development, developing the media is perceived as a necessary condition for other social goals to be achieved, even if the emphasis is on the former (Berger 2010: 549).

As a result of the blurred boundaries between media development and M4D, definitions of media development vary considerably – and confusingly. As the following two definitions illustrate, there are those which focus on the development of the media, and others which combine this with a focus on the role of the media in achieving other development goals.

> Media development generally refers to efforts by organizations, people, and sometimes governments to develop the capacity and quality of the media sector within a specific country or region. (CIMA 2013b)

> [Media development involves] empowering a multitude of media institutions and actors to operate independently and professionally, without undue constraints by the state or elites, promoting freedom of expression and democratic account-ability. (Kaufman 2012)

One of the tensions within the concept of media development, therefore, is whether it refers to an end in itself or whether it refers to the means to another end. This area of conceptual confusion is further compounded when media development, as an outcome, is conflated with other ultimate outcomes – for example, when indicators of media development are used as measures of democratic accountability (Berger 2010).

Responses to this apparent overlap between media develop-ment and M4D are varied. Warren Feek (2008) has argued that the distinction between the two is 'false and distracting' and should be abandoned altogether. He argues that it adds un-necessary confusion and detracts from the status of the broader field of communication and media for development. Instead, he points to common principles that unite the two approaches, such as a concern for improving an aspect of the human condition and the intersection of a communication process and a media form. By contrast, James Dean (cited in Alcorn et al. 2011: 13) has argued that it is 'more useful to see it ... [as] a continuum rather than a tired debate around media development and M4D'. Finally, Jo Weir (cited in ibid.: 12) contends that the distinction between the two terms is important and should be preserved, stating that, 'There is a huge difference between media development and media for development, and those two terms are often confused. It's a huge problem that people cannot differentiate between [them] ... It sometimes blurs the lines between journalism and advocacy.'

There is little doubt that media development and M4D are interlinked and complementary approaches which share many of the same principles (see GFMD 2005). Yet there remains a very real, if not absolute, distinction between them. The former focuses on achieving a particular media ecology and achieves its objectives through its very existence; the latter focuses on harnessing that system in an entirely instrumentalist way for pursuing discrete objectives, largely based on persuasion. Preserving and explaining this distinction is a vital part of understanding the various potential roles that the media have to play in international development. Perhaps what is required to combat this conceptual confusion is not the conflation of these terms, but greater conceptual precision through a more sophisticated terminology. Guy Berger (2010), for example, suggests that in order to avoid the conflation of ends and means when defining media development, we adopt the term 'media density' to describe the aim of deepening and increasing media's capacity to generate and circulate information.

It is worth pointing out, though, that while these two

approaches may appear to cover a wide range of ways in which media are linked – directly and indirectly – to development, in fact they both share a very narrow understanding of audiences and of their uses of media (Merkel 2012). They both generally assume that the most important forms of audience engagement with media are rational and deliberative responses to factual genres like news, current affairs and documentaries. Although the use of entertainment formats to provide educational content ('edutainment') is a common feature, particularly of M4D projects, the assumption is still that audiences will recognize and respond rationally to such content in ways that are directly related to development outcomes. While this particular function of the media can be significant, it represents only a very small part of the media's actual role in people's lives. Audiences engage with media for all sorts of reasons – to exchange gossip, to relax, to express themselves, to feel good about themselves, to build a sense of self – but perhaps most of all to be entertained. While these uses may or may not directly contribute to specific development outcomes, they are nevertheless all important in allowing audiences to live stimulating, fulfilling and enjoyable lives. The point is that the media have value well beyond their contribution to directed individual behaviour change or good governance and democracy (see Arora and Rangaswamy 2013). This is a fact generally overlooked or ignored by both M4D and media development initiatives.

External interventions or domestic initiatives?

Another key tension within the concept of media development emerges when the term is used to refer only to external interventions by international donors in a country's media sector (Berger 2010). For example, in a special report for the 2009

Salzburg Global Seminar on Supporting Independent Media (Glahn 2009: 1), media development is defined as 'a general term that refers to the various assistance programs *provided by international donors* and actors that offer economic, financial, technical and educational assistance to build and strengthen independent media' (emphasis added). Similarly, Berger (2010: 550) argues that 'even initiatives like the formation of Al Jazeera, despite being significant for gauging how "developed" Qatar's media system is, are not very often described as an example of "media development"'.

Focusing on media development as an external intervention is problematic because it obscures the central role of internal or indigenous developments within the media. This is important because the most successful examples of media development are widely agreed to be those driven by local governments and people, rather than donors. Tara Susman-Peña (2012: 47) argues that in Kenya, for example, most of the significant examples of media/ICT convergence and innovation have emerged from initiatives led by the media houses and telecom operators, rather than by donor agencies: 'Donors have supported innovation once they have identified initial successes, but they are not at the forefront, and they have not funded innovation themselves.'

Similarly, the recent expansion of right to information laws has been largely the result of long-running domestic campaigns driven by civil society, such as in the case of Thailand (see Chongkittavorn 2002).

An interventionist-based interpretation of media development also connects to a modernization view of development (see Chapter 1) in which the actions of donors are assumed to be the principal means by which countries in the global South are able to develop. This perspective is not helped by instances where donors are given the credit for successful locally driven examples of media development. In 'Rethinking media development' (Nelson and Susman-Peña 2012: 8), for example, grassroots movements for media development in countries like India, Mexico and South Africa are described as the 'blossoming' of 'seeds planted' by 'external players'. In India, however, the 2005 Right to Information Act was, to a significant degree, the achievement of the grassroots movement Mazdur Kisan Shakhti Sangathan (MKSS) (see Jenkins and Goetz 1999). This organization actually rejects institutional financial support and instead fund-raises among its grassroots supporters and relies on individual donations and revenue from MKSS 'fair price' shops.

In summary, defining media development as a purely donor-driven, intervention-based, activity obscures the most effective means by which sustainable media development is achieved and contributes to a patronizing view of development. In order to further distinguish between different meanings of the term media development, Berger (2010) suggests adopting the term 'media mobilization' to refer to external, intervention-based activities. This term, he suggests, is also less value laden and gets away from the problem that media development can denote intervention in a meddling or manipulative sense.

The affordances of different technologies within media development

A further complication regarding the concept of media development stems from the term 'media', which collapses all aspects of the media environment, ranging from professional journalism to mobile phone penetration, into one term. This unhelpfully obscures the various roles that different media can perform in media development and, in particular, obscures the unique affordances of new technologies.

In a review of the use of ICTs in media development

initiatives, Shanthi Kalathil (2008: 4) argues that donors have been slow to fully realize the potential of ICTs and those which have, 'tend to do so in the background, rather than making new technologies the major feature'. The dominant approach has been to simply incorporate new media technologies into traditional media development models. Examples of common practices in this regard include providing media outlets with updated equipment, using ICTs for distance learning for journalists, training journalists to use new technologies and creating online news platforms.

However, Kalathil (ibid.: 15) argues that simply 'digitizing' old models of media development is not enough. She suggests that 'new technologies have so fundamentally altered our collective sense of "the media," it seems reasonable to assume that the definition and categories of media development must shift as well'. Convergence, the emergence of citizen journalism, but also new forms of censorship and surveillance and threats to traditional business models have all affected, not only how the media operate, but inevitably how those wishing to promote media development should be working.

While it is difficult to pin down precisely what new, ICT-based models of media development might actually look like, there are certainly a number of questions we should be asking. To what extent should the field of media development converge with the field of 'ICT for development' (see Chapter 1), which is focused more on information delivery for behaviour change than on promoting democracy and good governance? In what ways should media development actors be involved in supporting citizen journalism or user-generated content creation more generally? Should the definition of an 'enabling environment' be extended to include a concern for access to the internet and mobile phones as well as telecommunications and internet law and policy? To what extent should assistance be directed at smaller grants focused on innovative, entrepreneurial-based ICT-related projects, rather than large, comprehensive, multi-year programmes focusing on the long-term development of the entire media sector (ibid.: 13)?

As was argued in Chapter 1, though, new technologies are certainly not a magic bullet. The effectiveness and appropriateness of ICT-related media development projects is constrained by a number of variables, including: lack of or unequal access to new technologies, potentially high initial costs, the prevalence of technical difficulties, dependence on a reliable power supply and/or network coverage, issues of long-term sustainability and/or dependence on suppliers and technical support, levels of technical literacy of the population and a lack of trust in non-familiar sources.

Whatever conclusion we ultimately reach about the role of ICTs in media development, this discussion has revealed the value of distinguishing between the affordances of different technologies within media development. It is for this reason that Berger (2010: 561) suggests disaggregating the meanings of the term 'media', so that we might, for example, identify 'journalism development' and 'ICT development' as subcategories of media development.

Measuring media development

It should be clear by this stage that the concept of media development defies easy definition because of the entanglement of activities and outcomes, the number of different factors it can include, the imprecise focus on domestic and/or donor activities and the various roles of different media. The final major issue regarding the notion of media development concerns its apparent universality, or the fact that it is often treated as a one-size-fits-all condition, applicable in all contexts. This is particularly apparent in attempts to evaluate or assess levels of media development.

There are three widely cited indices which are used to assess and compare the media environments of individual countries, at the macro-level.

- Since 1980 Freedom House has been publishing annual *Freedom of the Press* reports assessing the level of media independence in every country in the world. Levels of media freedom are scored on a scale from 1 (most free) to 100 (least free) and subsequently classified as either 'free', 'partly free' or 'not free'. This scoring and classification are based on the results of a set of twenty-three questions addressing the legal, political and economic environments of countries, answered by a team of regional experts and scholars and/or US-based Freedom House staff (Becker et al. 2007: 9).
- Launched in 2000, in cooperation with USAID, the IREX *Media Sustainability Index* (MSI) relies on local panels of media practitioners and related professionals to annually assess the conditions for independent media in eighty countries around the world. To measure media sustainability, five areas of media development are assessed: freedom of speech, professional journalism, plurality of news, business management and supporting institutions.
- The *Worldwide Press Freedom Index*, published by Reporters Without Borders, covers more than 179 countries and is designed to measure and rank countries according to their levels of press freedom only (rather than plurality or professionalism, for example). This annual index is constructed largely from the results of a questionnaire completed by journalists, researchers, jurists and human rights activists around the world. The survey asks questions specifically about direct

and indirect impediments to freedom of the press, including violence and intimidation.

Despite a strong reliance on these indicators by governments, donors, NGOs and researchers to track levels of media freedom, there is considerable debate about their value on grounds of reliability, applicability and universality. As Lee Becker, Tudor Vlad and Nancy Nusser (ibid.: 5) argue,

> The methodologies employed in creating these indices of media freedom are not always transparent ... and charges are often made about biases in the underlying assumptions behind them. Nor are the conceptual bases for the indices always obvious. It is possible that the competing indices measure different concepts, measure the same concept unreliably, or measure the same concepts in a reliable but invalid way.

Christina Holtz-Bacha (2004: 5) describes how the three categories Freedom House uses to assess press freedom are only roughly defined, very broad, differ considerably over time and 'do not lay open how the individual scores are actually reached'. Equally, since the Worldwide Press Freedom Index is based on individual perceptions, there can be significant differences between a country's ranking from one year to the next. These different indices are also all measuring very different aspects of media development. The Freedom of the Press report, for example, does not take into account the quality of the media or ethical standards of journalists (Coyne and Leeson 2009). As A. S. Panneerselvan and Lakshmi Nair (2008: 5) argue, while the data may give an indication of the state of the media environment, they fail to focus on the quality of work done by the media under severe constraints.

> The Reporters sans Frontières' Annual Press Freedom Index of 2005 lists Nepal among the worst ten countries with regard

to Press Freedom. It does not reflect how Nepal which was near the bottom of the pile as per 2005 surveys could in the same year, spark a successful People's Revolution to mark the country's transition from an authoritarian monarchy to a republic.

Despite this, these indices do generally reach similar findings and broadly agree with public opinion in each country (Becker et al. 2007). This adds weight to their apparent reliability. Furthermore, those who use these data are not blind to their methodological shortcomings and still find real value in them. As Mark Nelson (cited in Burgess 2010: 7) puts it, 'everybody knows that these numbers are not perfect and not without error ... You have to use caution in interpreting the data ... but they are really important and useful'.

The ideological basis of these different approaches generates the greatest area of critique. Christina Holtz-Bacha (2004: 2) argues that 'press freedom is understood differently in the various parts of the world ... even established democracies do not interpret press freedom in exactly the same way'. She points out, for example, that some media in Scandinavian countries, which are usually found at the top of the rankings, receive state subsidies or are controlled by political parties. For many, particularly in the USA, this would not meet their criteria for a free and independent press. The point is that, if what constitutes media development in any given context is determined very much by the particular conditions within a specific country, how can we develop standards of media development that are universal? Holtz-Bacha (ibid.: 9) concludes that

It is obvious that the indexes used for measuring freedom of the press have a Western bias. They mirror the norms and values of the highly developed Western democracies. Even more: These scales have a US bias. Therefore, they tend to reject any kind of media policy and to evaluate any activity by the state negatively, independent of its nature. Media ownership other than private is regarded with suspicion.

In the same vein, Banda (cited in Burgess 2010: 18) accuses Freedom House of having a 'neo-liberal predisposition towards the state as predatory, always encroaching on media freedom and independence'.

In support of this argument, Becker et al. (2007: 18) find that there is a higher correlation between the IREX and Freedom House's measures, which are both products of US organizations, compared to the Worldwide Press Freedom Index, which is produced by a French NGO. This, they suggest, 'at a minimum raises a question about the independence of the evaluations of country perspectives on press freedom reflecting domestic, political concerns'.

In response to such concerns over the ideological nature of these indices, African and Asian Media Barometers have been developed in an attempt to better reflect the conditions of particular regions of the world. The indicators for the African Media Barometer (AMB), for example, are said to derive, not from standards and ideals set out in Western countries, but from a number of existing multilateral standards developed on the African continent in the area of freedom of information and expression. These include the standards set out in the Windhoek Declaration (1991) and the Declaration on Principles of Freedom of Expression in Africa (2002). Thus, the African Media Barometer measures performance in media development against self-proclaimed continental standards, which helps to avoid accusations of Western bias (Banda and Berger 2009).

The process of self-assessment required by the AMB involves a panel of up to ten people, including media professionals and representatives of civil society groups (but not the government), meeting to debate and ultimately decide on the score (1 to 5) awarded to forty-five different indicators. These indicators are formulated as ideal goals within four sectors:

1. Freedom of expression, including freedom of the media, is effectively protected and promoted.
2. The media landscape is characterized by diversity, independence and sustainability.
3. Broadcasting regulation is transparent and independent; the state broadcaster is transformed into a truly public broadcaster.
4. The media operate according to high levels of professional standards.

The importance given to broadcasting, the transformation of the state broadcaster into a public broadcaster and an emphasis on a mix of private, public and community ownership are all examples of an attempt to 'Africanize' this index.

This attempt to focus on the regional peculiarities of media development stems from the argument that Western notions of media development may not be entirely relevant to African (or other) cultural realities. One of the most famous advocates of this perspective is Francis Nyamnjoh (2005: 27), who argues that there is an inherent conflict between traditional African loyalties to social and ethnic groups and journalistic principles of independence and impartiality.

If African philosophies of personhood and agency stress interdependence between individual and the community and between communities, and if journalists identify with any of the many cultural communities seeking recognition and representation at local and national levels, they are bound to be torn between serving their community and serving the 'imagined' rights-bearing, autonomous individual 'citizens' of the liberal democratic model. A democracy that stresses independence, in a situation where both the world-view and the material realities emphasise interdependence, is bound to result only in dependence. The contradictions of and multifaceted pressures on the media are a perfect reflection of such tensions and a pointer to the need for domesticated ideas of democracy in Africa.

In a counter-view, Berger (2011: 1) asserts that journalistic values of independence, pluralism and freedom *are* universal.

The idealism that powers [African journalists'] work is not a Western concern, even if it is shared in much of the West. Instead, it is a universal driver of why people choose to become journalists in the first place. It transcends various national or continental journalisms (in the plural) – i.e. various cultural forms and traditions of journalism.

It is in this context that John Burgess (2010: 23) argues that 'all in all, it's hard to point to many assumptions and values in the African Media Barometer that are uniquely "African"'.

In summary, it should be clear that there are no easy answers to the questions of how to measure media development and whether or not there are any universal dimensions to it. Universal indices struggle to deal with the issue of a lack of international consensus on what media development actually is. Attempts to compensate for this by regionalizing indicators are themselves accused of obscuring universal characteristics of media development. For my part, I would argue that such debates about measurement and universality are made even more challenging by the broader conceptual confusion that surrounds the idea of media development. As Lee Becker and Tudor Vlad put it, 'it is hard to measure something if you do not know exactly what it is' (cited in ibid.: 8). Outlining the key features of media development and the main areas of contestation is an important first step, perhaps not to resolving these debates, but at least to making them more transparent.

Conclusion

It should be clear by now that because of the many different interpretations and elements of media development, attempting to define the term can feel a bit like nailing jelly to a wall. The aim here has been to produce a clearer understanding of this important but slippery concept by outlining the key contours and tensions within the field.

This discussion has also highlighted many of the key questions to be asked when pursuing media development interventions. In any given context, we need to consider what dimensions of media development should be prioritized, based on a comprehensive understanding of local circumstances. When allocating finite resources, should the focus be on short-term journalist training, or long-term efforts to enhance the enabling environment, for example? How important is economic sustainability? It is also important to ask: on what basis are these decisions being made? What normative premises do we carry about the role media *should* play in society? To what extent is it a pragmatic decision, based on the capacity of donor organizations to deliver and account for their work, rather than on an assessment of local needs? Are we guilty of assuming that what works in one context is equally relevant in other contexts?

To what extent is it appropriate to integrate new technologies into a project? In fact, should we be integrating new technologies into conventional projects at all, or actually changing the way we think about media development interventions altogether? Is media development being understood as an end in itself or a means to achieving something else? How should success be measured: in terms of the activities completed, or the outcomes they achieve? What assumptions are carried by the indicators we use to evaluate projects? How can media development interventions complement the work of M4D-based projects and vice versa? Perhaps most importantly – how can donor-based interventions be integrated into the work of local initiatives?

If media development interventions are to be made as effective as possible, it is important to fully understand the many choices that need to be made, as well as the implications of each decision. In a complex area such as this, the guiding principle for donors and policy-makers should be to 'thoroughly understand media and politics in a given country before intervening' and to 'do no harm' (Myers 2012b: 8).

4 | From Media Development to Development: A Long and Winding Road

If the focus in the last chapter was on what media development is, the central question addressed in this chapter is: why develop the media? Even if we accept that the aim of media development is distinct from the instrumentalist agenda of media for development (M4D), it remains the case that media development is linked, in some ways, to development. The question is – how?

Answers to this question are, unfortunately, often rather abstract, confusing or idealistic. One of the most famous statements about the case for supporting media as a critical component of development is the following comment by former World Bank president James Wolfensohn (1999):

> A free press is not a luxury. A free press is at the absolute core of equitable development, because if you cannot enfranchise poor people, if they do not have a right to expression, if there is no searchlight on corruption and inequitable practices, you cannot build the public consensus needed to bring about change.

It is not immediately clear, however, how a 'searchlight on corruption' leads to the building of consensus. Or indeed whether consensus is always the result of 'enfranchising poor people'. We might also wonder whether, in fact, public consensus is an effective mechanism for change in any context other than a fully functioning democracy.

What is perhaps most revealing about this statement, therefore, is precisely the fact that it fails to pin down the direct causal role of media development for development. Indeed, the central argument in this chapter is that the connections between media development and key aspects of development, including good governance, democracy and economic development, are multiple, complex and contingent upon local circumstances.

Moreover, it is revealing that Wolfensohn's statement is so well cited, presumably not because of its clarity in explaining the causal role of the media, but because the case for media development is being made by such a prominent figure in mainstream development. An additional theme of this chapter is that seeking to highlight the importance of media development, in the face of its ongoing marginalization, should not be allowed to get in the way of developing a critical understanding of the complexities and contingencies of its relationship with development. Anecdotes, rhetoric and uncritical reviews of evidence are not a solid basis for building the case for a more significant and sustained engagement with the media. While the first half of this chapter focuses on critically reviewing the role of media development in good governance, democracy and economic development, in the second half, the intrinsic value of developed media is discussed alongside a political economy perspective on media development and the role of community media.

Democracy, good governance and media development

Providing support for the media, whether by enhancing independence, plurality, professionalism, capacity, financial sustainability or media literacy, is based on the premise that independent media have a central role to play in supporting democracy and good governance. This argument has a very well-established history in the work of liberal theorists such as John Milton, John Locke and John Stuart Mill (Keane 1991). For example, John Stuart Mill (2003 [1859]) made the case for press freedom on the grounds that airing all views is the only real means of attaining truth. From a theological basis, John Milton (1644) argued that press freedom was vital for allowing man to choose between good and evil. From the perspective of individual rights, John Locke (1689) argued that press freedom guaranteed liberty from the political elite.

More recently, Pippa Norris (2010) has produced one of the most well-cited accounts, which draws on this liberal tradition to attempt to explain why media development impacts upon good governance and democracy. In brief, she argues that the ideal roles of the news media are 'as watchdogs over the powerful; as agenda setters, calling attention to natural and human-caused disasters and humanitarian crises; and as gatekeepers, incorporating a diverse and balanced range of political perspectives and social sectors' (ibid.: 5). Each of these claims is worth explaining in detail as they form the basis of most contemporary accounts of the significance of media development.

The watchdog function In traditional liberal arguments about the democratic role of the press, the primary function of the media is to act as a public watchdog – scrutinizing the activities of the state and other sources of power. According to this well-known ideal, the media should guard the public interest, protecting it from incompetence, corruption and misinformation by promoting transparency and accountability among the powerful (Norris 2008). It is in this context that the media are described as the 'fourth estate', providing a check and balance on the powerful in society – counterbalancing the power of the executive, legislative and judiciary (Norris and Odugbemi

2010a: 16). This is the primary logic behind the need for the media to be independent from the government – because once the media become subject to regulation the assumption is that they will lose their ability to be critical of those with power. This is also the logic that drove the First Amendment to the US Constitution and which continues to underpin the deregulation of broadcasting in the USA.

This watchdog role can be fulfilled through the work of investigative journalism, which can expose maladministration by public officials, corruption in the judiciary or scandals in the corporate sector (Donohue et al. 2006). Recent examples of this in the UK include the 2009 parliamentary expenses scandal and the 2011 News International phone-hacking scandal being revealed by the *Telegraph* and the *Guardian* newspapers respectively. To provide evidence of the importance of the media in this regard, compared to other democratic checks and balances, John McMillan and Pablo Zoido (2004) examined the amount of money paid to 'buy off' different institutions during Alberto Fujimori's rule in Peru in the 1990s. Based on an analysis of the carefully kept records of the chief of secret police, Vladimiro Montesinos Torres, they find that television-channel owners were, on average, paid around one hundred times more than judges or politicians. If the amount paid is taken as a reflection of the government's view of the importance of each restraint, then we can conclude that, in this case, television was perceived to be the most effective mechanism of accountability – even more so than newspapers. Moreover, this concern for television turned out to be well justified. Montesinos had chosen not to pay off Channel N – a relatively small subscription-based satellite channel, with a market share of less than 5 per cent. Yet in September 2000, it was this station that showed a videotape of Montesinos bribing an opposition political leader to support President Fujimori – which turned out to be the catalyst for the Fujimori government's eventual downfall. It is examples such as this which have reinvigorated the notion of the media as watchdog, particularly in the context of societies emerging from authoritarian rule.

The media can also fulfil their role of watchdog in a more neutral way, by providing routine, timely and accurate information about public affairs. This can help citizens to monitor the performance of governments in delivering basic services, for example. One of the most famous studies to provide empirical support to this claim is an analysis by Ritva Reinikka and Jakob Svensson (2004) of the apparent effect that newspaper publication of Uganda's education budget had on reducing corruption. In an effort to reduce the capture of government subsidies to primary schools, the Ugandan government launched an information campaign in 1995, largely through newspapers, to make teachers and parents aware of their school's entitlement to government grants. During the period of this information campaign, the amount of money reaching individual schools increased from an average of 24 per cent of the grant in 1995, to 80 per cent in 2001. To investigate the role of newspapers in this marked decline in corruption, Reinikka and Svensson compared schools' proximity to a newspaper outlet with its change in funding. They found that schools with access to newspapers increased their funding by an average of 14 per cent more than schools that lacked access to newspapers. They conclude that 'a strong relationship exists between proximity to a newspaper outlet and reduction in capture' (ibid.: 1).

Setting aside questions regarding the possibility of the media fulfilling such a watchdog function, there are real limitations to claims which unproblematically link media freedom directly to good governance and democracy in this way. Primarily, we must recognize that the media's impact is contingent upon other actors and processes. For investigative journalism to be effective, for example, it is not enough to simply expose wrongdoing. Other mechanisms of accountability, such as the judiciary, parliament and civil society, need to act if the powerful are to be held accountable. In Peru, for example, while Channel N may have circulated evidence of the Fujimori government's corruption, it was the ability of the public and the political opposition to mobilize against the regime which directly caused its downfall. Similarly, Reinikka and Svensson acknowledge that in Uganda it would be wrong to attribute the reduction in capture of government grants to the newspaper campaign alone (despite some interpretations of this study doing so – see Collier 2007: 150). Indeed, during the period of the campaign there were significant changes in the size, accounting and method of delivery of these grants, which may also have affected levels of corruption. Reinikka and Svensson's research tells us only that the media had some role to play, rather than precisely what role they played or their precise degree of importance.

Moreover, the media often do not act alone in exposing wrongdoing. In the USA, for example, government investigators and Congress supported journalists in uncovering the Watergate scandal (Schudson 1992). In the case of the Ugandan example, it was the Ugandan government itself which made use of the media to tackle corruption. Thus, while the watchdog role of the media may help to promote democratic accountability, so the institutional arrangements of democracy provide a hospitable environment for watchdog reporting (Coronel 2010). As John Street (2010: 271) puts it, 'democratic media do not, in and of themselves, create democracy. Democratic media need a democratic polity, and vice versa.'

The question of whether the media's watchdog function always *contributes* to democracy and good governance, or whether there are circumstances where it might *detract* from it, has also been asked. This thought is at the heart of the so-called Asian

Model of media development in which some degree of state control over the press is seen as necessary for avoiding division and achieving common societal objectives. Former Singaporean prime minister Goh Chok Tong, for example, argued that 'Having our media play the role as the fourth estate cannot be the starting point for building a stable, secure, incorrupt, and prosperous Singapore. The starting point is how to put in place a good government to run a clean, just and efficient system' (cited in Burgess 2010: 18).

Similarly, former Chinese president Hu Jintao has stated that the proper role of media is to 'use their distinctive assets and advantages to convey the messages of peace, development, cooperation, mutual benefit, and tolerance' (cited in People's Daily 2009). In support of this idea, Norris and Inglehart (2010: 215) have found that levels of citizens' confidence in their government are significantly higher in societies with restrictive rather than pluralistic media environments.

Equally, media malaise theories posit that the ceaseless criticism of politics and politicians erodes public trust and support for government institutions, making it more difficult to govern effectively (Coronel 2010). In particular, it is often suggested that aggressive and critical reporting of the governments of countries that have only recently become democratic can damage the public's support for democracy itself. Indeed, in many transition societies, accusations of corruption played out in the media are part of the arsenal of political contestation (ibid.), which, even if it does not damage public support for democracy, does serve to focus political discourse on sleaze and scandal rather than other issues of importance (Sajo 2003).

The aim here is not to debate the extent to which a watchdog function is beneficial in different societies. Rather, it is to highlight that the causal relationship between the media's watchdog role and democracy and good governance is more complicated and contingent than it is often presented as being. The precise magnitude, direction and nature of this relationship depend very much on context, and particularly on the nature of democracy in a given country.

Agenda-setting and the media The central premise of agenda-setting theory is that the media have the ability to influence the salience of topics on the public agenda (McCombs and Reynolds 2002). Put another way, while media cannot tell us what to think (see Chapter 1) they can help to set the agenda of what we think about. Unlike for direct effects theories of media effects, there is much empirical support for this view of the influence of the media.

In the context of the media's role in democracy and good governance, agenda-setting refers to the media's function in highlighting the importance of particular social issues for the public and politicians (Norris 2010: 17). Norris (2008: 69) argues that during urgent humanitarian crises in particular, independent reporters can act as a vital channel of information for decision-makers, helping to make democratic governments more responsive to the needs of the people. In order for the media to fulfil this agenda-setting function they must have the capacity and willingness to seek out and publish this information. The media must also be free from the influence of those sources of power whose interests may be served by the concealment of these issues. In other words, the media must have achieved a certain level of media development. Where the media do not have such freedoms, important social issues can remain concealed, to the detriment of society. For example, during the SARS (Severe Acute Respiratory Syndrome) outbreak in 2002, the Chinese government initially suppressed reporting of the epidemic, fearing that such 'negative' news could cause unrest and damage China's image (Kalathil 2003). This lack of information allegedly caused delays in efforts to control the epidemic and uninformed citizens may have continued risky behaviours that spread the disease (Hume 2005: 4).

This agenda-setting role has its roots in a 'consumer representation' view of the media in traditional liberal theory, whereby, in a free market, the media are understood to represent the needs of the people to those in power (Curran 2000). The assumption is that, in a free market, newspapers are subject to the equivalent of an election every time they go on sale. They therefore serve as a daily reflection of public opinion because readers are assumed to buy newspapers that best fit their political opinions. Consequently, 'the media as a whole reflect the views and values of the buying public and act as a public mouth piece' (ibid.: 91). In this view, the media play a vital role of channelling citizens' concerns to decision-makers in government by providing information about urgent social problems.

Easily the most well-cited claim in support of this agenda-setting function of the media is Amartya Sen's (1999) assertion that no famine has ever occurred in a country with a free press. Drawing on examples from India, Sen (ibid.: 181) argues that a free press acts as an early-warning system for countries threatened by famines by providing information which a government might wish to suppress.

> The most elementary source of basic information from distant areas about a threatening famine are enterprising news media, especially when there are incentives – provided by a democratic system – for bringing out facts that may be embarrassing to the government (facts that an authoritarian government would tend to censor out). (Ibid.: 87)

To illustrate his point, Sen contrasts the situation in India with that of China during the 1959–61 famine, in which between 20 and 43 million people are estimated to have been killed and where media coverage was tightly controlled under Chairman Mao's rule.

Empirical support for this theoretical claim is provided by the work of Timothy Besley and Robin Burgess (2002) in a study of how the governments of all of India's sixteen states varied in their responses to food shortages, between 1958 and 1992. They find that the states which were most responsive to food crises were not wealthier states, but those with higher levels of newspaper circulation, especially in local languages: '[A] 1 percent increase in newspaper circulation is associated with a 2.4 percent increase in public food distribution and a 5.5 percent increase in calamity relief expenditures' (ibid.: 1435).

This, they suggest, is the result of electorates altering their voting behaviours based on information provided by independent, local-language newspapers regarding politicians' records in responding to food crises.

While this provides another seemingly logical and compelling example of the direct causal link between media development and good governance, there are a number of qualifications to Sen's argument, and to the agenda-setting role of the media in general, which help to produce a more nuanced account of the role of the media. First, it is not always clear who is setting whose agenda. In the consumer representation argument, public demand is the driving force of media content, which subsequently influences elites. By contrast, in a pure agenda-setting version of this argument, the news media are seen as acting independently, exerting influence on both the public and, often through them, on politicians. In alternative views, the media are seen as responding to competing elite priorities or as being governed by world events.

Secondly, Sen makes clear that this early-warning function of the media can operate only in a properly functioning electoral system with viable opposition parties. As with the watchdog function, the information provided by the media will not be effective without supporting institutions, such as political competition, so that incumbents can be voted out of office, for example. In short, the point is that the relationship between media development and democracy and good governance is two-way.

Finally, the precise role of the media depends very much on the political and media environment of the country. Sen's argument, for example, assumes conditions in which the population is heavily dependent on the state for social protection, as in India (Myers 2012b). It also refers only to *major* famines. Narasimhan Ram (1995: 173) points out that while the Indian press may be good at covering large-scale, dramatic crises, they are not good at covering chronic hunger – the coverage of which he describes as 'low key, tame and ... frequently incompetent'.

In summary, a free press may be important in performing an agenda-setting role but it is not the only condition sufficient for the prevention of famines, for example, and the precise means by which it functions is often far from clear. As Norris (2010: 387) herself recognizes, 'this is a complex interaction, and considerable care is needed to disentangle the precise timeline involved in the agenda-setting process, to establish who leads and who follows in the dance'.

The media as civic forum Norris (ibid.: 18) describes the third major role of the media as being to serve as a space where journalists and broadcasters bring together a plurality of diverse interests, political parties, viewpoints and social sectors to debate issues of public concern. This once again draws on classic liberal arguments, this time about the media acting as a public sphere (Habermas 1989). The public sphere is a normative vision of a public space in which public opinion is formed which supervises government. Is it characterized by freely available access to information, discussion that is free from interference by the state and by equality and mutual respect among groups and individuals. The media's role is to provide an arena for the establishment of a consensus among the public, based on reason and rational deliberation, which can shape the direction of government policy. As Paul Collier (2008: 2) has put it, 'in terms of good policy, the media is absolutely critical ... if the government does not happen to get it right – which it probably won't – then somebody in the broader society has to be articulating, critiquing, and proposing alternative views – educating the government'.

While this may be an idealistic vision and Habermas's characterization of the public sphere has been criticized for being historically inaccurate and overlooking questions of social exclusion (see Mouffe 1999), it frequently serves as model of how the media should function in a democracy. Indeed, the links between media's role in establishing a public sphere and democracy and good governance are reasonably clear (at least in theory). In a liberal democracy, the formation of policy should be a rational and deliberative process that takes into account the concerns and interests of all groups. The establishment of a free space to facilitate this process is vital for achieving this. The provision of inclusive opportunities for the participation and representation of all members of society in the media is a particularly important aspect of free and fair elections. Citizens can make informed choices about whom they vote for only if opposition parties, candidates and groups have fair access to the media.

As evidence of the importance of a public sphere in development, the results of a World Bank (1999) survey of 40,000 people in 1999 found that, when asked what they desired most, 'having a voice' was one of the most frequent replies, second only to improved income and basic necessities. Not being able to have a say in decisions that affect their lives was identified as a key element of poverty in itself (Wilson and Warnock

2007: 8). The authors of a similar World Bank (2001) report on the results of a survey of 20,000 poor people in twenty-three countries concluded that

> [What most] differentiates poor people from rich people is a lack of voice. The inability to be represented. The inability to convey to the people in authority what it is that they think. The inability to have a searchlight put on the conditions of inequality. These people interviewed do not have Ph.D.s but they have the knowledge of poverty, and the first thing they talked about is not money. It is lack of voice, it is lack of the ability to express themselves.

However, as with all claims about the direct links between media and democracy/good governance, there are a number of ways in which seemingly logical theoretical arguments can be quite easily problematized. There is an assumption in this particular argument that public debate is always rational and that it necessarily produces logical and informed consensus on an issue. Yet in reality, public debate is not always rational and facilitating an open space of discussion is no guarantee of calm debate and consensus, rather than a polarization of views, increased animosity and illogical and emotional decision-making.

Disagreement about the potential consequences of open public debate is particularly apparent in the context of fragile states. Norris and Odugbemi (2010a: 20) argue that the role of the media in providing a civic forum is 'perhaps most critical in post-conflict states and deeply divided societies, as a way of encouraging dialogue, tolerance, and interaction among diverse communities, reducing the underlying causes of conflict, and building the conditions for a lasting peace'. Similarly, Mark Harvey (2007: 7) argues that 'healthy public spheres can host a wide range of views which can dilute intolerance'. The assumption in such arguments is that the best way to counter divisive speech is to allow for more speech, so that multiple perspectives are available, rather than to impose restrictions. This is based upon the principle of the 'marketplace of ideas' in the liberal tradition, whereby the competition of ideas in an open and transparent public sphere is assumed to result in the emergence of truth or, in this context, moderate or balanced discourse. As Abraham Lincoln is claimed to have said, 'let the people know the facts, and the country will be safe'.

The most striking challenge to this assumption comes from the apparent role that the liberalization of the media had in the Rwanda genocide in 1994. The power-sharing agreement between the Hutus and the Tutsis the year before (the Arusha Accords) involved significant liberalization of the media, based on the assumption that a more open public sphere would promote a more balanced discourse. However, this resulted in the rapid creation of numerous news media outlets, largely dominated by extreme voices, often broadcasting highly inaccurate and overtly biased editorials (Allen and Stremlau 2005: 222). One of these new outlets was the infamous Milles Collines radio station, which is now generally accepted to have played a key role in inciting and organizing the genocide (Thompson 2007). Drawing on this and other examples, Tim Allen and Nicole Stremlau (2005) argue that in such circumstances 'a degree of censorship may be essential ... where establishing a political framework is vital to peace building'. Similarly, James Putzel and Joost van der Zwan (2005: 1) argue that

> In situations where the state is fragile ..., and where the
> political process is unstable and de-legitimated, the primary
> objective of donor assistance should be supporting the forma-
> tion of a functioning state. In such a scenario, unsophisticated
> liberalisation of the media can potentially undermine the state
> building project.

As with so much of the literature on media development, there is an assumption that the media are working at optimal performance, i.e. as in Western democracies. Putzel (2010) makes this point clear when he recommends that 'it can never be appropriate for donors to promote media without understanding the country context. To do otherwise is to violate the "do no harm" principle.'

In each of these three visions of the role of a free press in society – watchdog, agenda-setting and civic forum – it is possible to make a strong and seemingly logical case to explain how media development can directly contribute to good governance and democracy. Yet it has also been demonstrated that these seemingly logical arguments can in fact mask complex lines of causality and the importance of context.

Empirical evidence linking media development to democracy and good governance

There is now a wealth of statistical research, using country-level data, which supports the existence of a link between media development and indicators of democracy and good governance. Some of the most prominent or compelling studies include the following:

- Stephan Armah and Loyd Amoah (2010) present the results of one of many studies which claim to provide strong empirical evidence that a lack of press freedom is strongly associated with higher levels of corruption, in this case in sub-Saharan African countries.
- Sanghamitra Bandyopadhyay (2009) finds that levels of newspaper, radio and television penetration in a country have a robust negative association with both corruption and inequality.

- In 'Giving voice to the voiceless', Pippa Norris and Dieter Zinnbauer (2002: 2) find, rather strikingly, that 'media systems characterized by widespread mass access *and* by an independent press … experience less corruption, greater administrative efficiency, higher political stability, and more effective rule of law, as well as better development outcomes such as higher per capita income, greater literacy, less economic inequality, lower infant mortality rates, and greater public spending on health'.

- Using spatial econometric techniques and a sample of 102 countries, Russell Sobel, Nabamita Dutta and Sankukta Roy (2010) find evidence to support a conclusion that an expansion of a country's level of media freedom prompts an increase of approximately 25 per cent in the media freedom of neighbouring countries.

Despite indicating the existence of a strong and significant positive correlation between media development and good governance and democracy, the results of such studies have very real limitations. Most importantly, such statistical analyses cannot account for *why* or *how* media development is linked to these particular aspects of development. They cannot, for example, establish which function of the press is most important – watchdog, agenda-setter or civic forum, or indeed, any alternative function. These studies also fail to explain the existence of important exceptions, such as Singapore, which is widely regarded as having relatively low levels of corruption despite restrictions on press freedom (Norris and Odugbemi 2010b). Similarly, they fail to account for the fact that countries like Colombia, Portugal and Ukraine can all have similar measures of democracy but quite different measures of press freedom (Islam 2002a).

Furthermore, Norris (2008) herself recognizes that these analyses are not particularly helpful in disentangling some of the *reciprocal* relationships between the government and the media which may be at work. As argued above, media development may have a role to play in promoting good governance and democracy but so too does the advancement of good governance and democratization have a role to play in enabling media development. Thus, the existence of strong positive correlations between these variables does not explain which causes the other. This ambiguity is revealed in the use of terms such as 'associated with', 'tied to' and 'strong association between', which signal a connection, but not the nature of causality.

In summary, existing empirical evidence adds weight to the theoretical case that media development matters, but the issue remains that it cannot be isolated from or held solely responsible for good governance and democratization. What is required to flesh out the role of media development more fully is more detailed, qualitative case-study work in different contexts.

Media development and economic development

The same pattern of explanations, evidence and limitations can be found in claims regarding the link between media development and economic growth. There are many examples of statistical analyses which provide evidence to support a strong positive correlation between countries with well-developed economies and a free press. As far back as 1960, Raymond Nixon (1960) found that per capita national income was positively related to the level of press freedom. More recently, the World Bank (see Wolfensohn 1999) and others (Djankov et al. 2002) have produced similar studies. Wolfensohn (1999) summarizes studies at the World Bank that show 'there is a strong positive correlation between voice and accountability and measures such as per capita income'. This evidence of correlation is tied to a range of explanations, following the same basic arguments as above, about the possible (and often direct) causal role that free and independent media apparently play in economic development.

One of the most often cited claims concerns the importance for economic development of the availability of information in individual decision-making. Just as the public requires accurate and reliable information to make informed political decisions, e.g. in deciding whom to vote for, so in economic markets, consumers need accurate and reliable information to compare and evaluate products and services to make the most informed economic decisions (Stiglitz 2002). The value of the role of the media in spreading accurate, timely and accessible economic information is often illustrated with the idea that it can help small producers to participate in markets on more equal terms. New communications technologies in particular are increasingly being promoted as a means of enabling small farmers to get more accurate market price information, thus putting them in a stronger position for negotiating the prices for their goods (Wilson and Warnock 2007). The use of anecdotal examples to support this idea is a key characteristic of this literature.

> In the village of Wu'an in Hebei Province, farmer Li Suotian received continually updated market information. He found out that Israeli breeds of tomatoes sold well in Hebei. He then grew more than 1 mu (0.07 hectares) of tomatoes and obtained an annual income of 3,500 yuan (US$421) from them. That income was eight times his normal income from grain growing. (Colle 2007: 217)

Beyond providing accurate market price information to make economies run more efficiently and fairly, the media can also help farmers to know

What and when to plant; where to find agricultural inputs at the best price; how to identify and respond to disease, pests and droughts; where to sell products, what new technology options exist for production, post-harvest and soil fertility control; and what agricultural credit and other government programmes are available. (Ibid.: 101)

Many of the claims about the role of a free press in serving as a watchdog or civic forum can also be connected to improvements in economic governance. For example, in their analysis of the role of the media in the economic transitions of Hungary and Poland, Christopher Coyne and Peter Leeson (2009) argue that, in both cases, open and free media fostered greater transparency and inclusion in the economic policy-making process, which resulted in more inclusive and effective economic policies. In their review of this, and other, research, Arsenault and Powers (2010: 22) add that 'successful economic development is, at its core, characterized by widespread coordination, and … effective coordination between various political and social actors is best facilitated through a free media'.

The media are also central to the creative industries, which can be closely tied to economic development through income generation and job creation. In Jamaica, for example, music is one of the highest-earning exports, with beneficial spin-offs in other sectors such as tourism (Locksley 2008: 11). In Nigeria, the Nollywood film industry is reported to be the second-biggest employer, after agriculture (ibid.: 11). In India, the Bollywood film industry has an annual turnover of several billion US dollars.

As argued earlier, however, the existence of statistical correlations and logical theoretical explanations is not sufficient to demonstrate a clear role for media development in economic development. For example, the direction of causality is not necessarily from media to economic growth. As Roumten Islam (2002a: 8) argues,

How non-media industries are structured and the government's overall economic policies have significant effects on the media's independence and performance ... Even privatizing the media industry will not solve the problems of bias if the only advertisers, and thus the financiers, are state-owned enterprises.

Indeed, in the early quantitative studies of the link between press freedom and economic development, causality was understood to operate in the opposite direction. 'For it long has been apparent, as Schramm suggests, that a particular kind of press ... can develop only to the extent that certain variables – socioeconomic, cultural and otherwise – make it possible' (Nixon 1960: 13).

More specifically, David Weaver (1977) provided evidence to support the suggestion that increases in economic productivity lead to less stress in the political system, which leads to increased press freedom.

There are also many examples of countries experiencing significant economic growth without media freedom. As Mushtaq Khan (cited in Lines 2009) points out, in China, the fastest economic growth in human history occurred without a free press. Paul Siu-nam Lee (1994) describes China as having adopted a 'pragmatic approach' to press freedom, on the basis that maintaining social stability and building consensus is important for economic growth. This mirrors the claims of Wilbur Schramm (1964), often referred to as the father of communication studies, who argued that state control over the media was the most effective means of achieving economic development because it can 'emphasize collective ends rather than individual freedoms'.

The task of the mass media ... is to speed and ease the long, slow social transformation required for economic development, and, in particular, to speed and smooth the task of mobilizing human resources behind the national effort. This mobilizing of human resources requires a great deal of attention to what the population knows and thinks of national development. (Ibid.: 8)

There are, however, important questions about the sustainability of this pattern of press control and economic development. Nelson and Susman-Peña (2012: 18) argue that 'Chinese analysts seem to agree that the country will have to continue progressively opening its media sector for China to maintain its economic growth'.

Once again, the aim here is not to debate whether media freedom necessarily enhances or inhibits economic development. Rather, it is to demonstrate that the causal role of the media in relation to economic growth is far more messy, complicated and contingent than is often presented. Having applied this argument in several different contexts now, we move to reviewing alternative ways of thinking about the importance of media development.

'We communicate, therefore we are' (Panneer-selvan and Nair 2008)

Given the difficulties in isolating the causal role of media development in development, perhaps a more productive approach to understanding the value of media development is to highlight its intrinsic, rather than (or as well as) its instrumental, value. In *Development as Freedom*, Sen (1999) suggests that expanding human freedoms is both the means and the goal of development. In this approach, the expansion of freedom of expression through media development can be seen as important, both as a means for achieving development outcomes, such as democratization and economic development, and also as an outcome in itself. As Guy Berger (2010: 557) argues, 'certain kinds of media performance are not just a means to democracy, but an essential part of the definition of democracy'. Similarly, Mary Myers (2012b: 8) argues that 'Contexts may vary, but the case for press freedom is based on the universal right to freedom of expression, and this still stands, irrespective of whether or not the effects of media are "positive" or "negative" from a governance perspective.'

The guarantee of freedom of expression and information is regarded as a basic human right in the Universal Declaration of Human Rights, the European Convention on Human Rights, the American Convention on Human Rights, and the African Charter on Human and Peoples' Rights (see Norris and Zinnbauer 2002). Article 19 of the Universal Declaration of Human Rights (1948) states that 'everyone has the right to freedom of opinion and expression; this right includes freedom to hold opinions without interference and to seek, receive, and impart information and ideas through any media regardless of frontiers'.

Yet even the idea that freedom of expression is a human right, which the media can help to promote, is not without controversy. In the 1970s, this idea was at the heart of highly charged global debates about the role of international communications flows in maintaining unequal power relations. The right to freedom of expression, it was alleged, privileges the powerful because without equal attention to ensuring equality in the *means* to communicate, those with most power will always be able to shout the loudest.

A poor person seeking to highlight injustice in their lives and a powerful media mogul each have, before the law, precisely the same protection for their right to freely express their views. In practice, however, the former lacks a means to have her/his voice heard, while the latter can powerfully amplify her/his message (WACC 2005: 2).

Applied to the level of international relations, the principle of free flow of information means that those countries with a more developed media will likely dominate global communication flows and benefit from them. Indeed, in the 1970s and 1980s up to 90 per cent (New Internationalist 1981) of the entire foreign news output of the world's newspapers was produced by just four different news agencies. Each major international news agency was associated with one of the dominant powers at the time, including Associated Press (USA), United Press International (USA), Agence France-Presse (France), Reuters (UK) and the Telegraph Agency of the Soviet Union (USSR). Non-aligned countries alleged that because the news content was designed to suit domestic audiences and the entry costs of setting up a competing service were so high, they were forced to rely on news which had minimal coverage of issues relevant to them. Moreover, when non-aligned countries were covered, they were reported through a Western lens, resulting in the reinforcing of stereotypes, a lack of historical and social context and a focus on either violence and disasters or trivial issues.

The more general idea of the media of one country being subject to substantial pressure from the media interests of another country, and that this is implicated in the extension of unequal power relations between states, was referred to as media imperialism (Boyd-Barrett 1977). At the time, complaints about media imperialism and the consequences of unequal flows of information led to demands from non-aligned countries for a New World Information and Communications Order (NWICO). The response from Western countries was to allege that demands for a NWICO were an excuse for maintaining government control of media – and the USA and the UK pulled out of UNESCO, where these debates had raged.

In more recent years, the rise of globalization, multiple centres of production and new technologies have fundamentally transformed the directions and magnitude of the flow of communications between countries, upon which demands for a NWICO were based (Straubhaar 2000). Furthermore, the lack of conceptual precision and inaccurate assumptions about audiences and media effects led to the increasing irrelevance of the concept of media imperialism. Despite this, though, the more general idea that the structure of global communications is interwoven with the exercise of power remains important (Thompson 1995: 166). Debates about media imperialism and the NWICO remind us that media development can be seen, not just as a means of promoting democracy and good governance within a society, but also as being implicated in the contesting of global relations of power on the international stage.

Equally, such debates remind us that pursuing a more developed media system as a means of promoting democracy and good governance is not the only way of interpreting the process of media development. For example, adopting a political economy perspective, Manyozo (2012: 151) describes dominant media development practices as 'an instrument of modernisation'. He argues that a neoliberal market economy model of civil society, which has been successful at consolidating democracy and good governance in the West, is being transplanted uncritically in the global South, partly through media development interventions, with the assumption that it is equally appropriate. Yet this approach disregards the importance of indigenous knowledge communication systems (IKCS) and hybrid or traditional governance systems, which often exist alongside Western models. Moreover, Manyozo suggests that the action of consolidating market-friendly models of media systems in the global South contributes to an overdependence on external aid, reinforces minority power structures within the country and ultimately serves transnational/corporate interests. Thus, while media development may indeed be understood as a defence against media imperialism, if we are sympathetic to Manyozo's argument, then dominant media development practices might also be interpreted as actively contributing to a new form of media imperialism.

Community media

Vibrant community-based media have come to be regarded as a vital part of a healthy, developed media system in recent years (UNESCO 2008) and supporting community media has certainly become a priority for many donors and policy-makers working in media development. Across Africa, community radio grew, on average, by 1,386 per cent between 2000 and 2006 (Kaplan 2012: 117). But what exactly are community media and how do they relate to media development and to development?

Manyozo (2012: 115) suggests that a community development approach to media development is distinct from the dominant – good governance – strand of media development, discussed in this chapter, in a number of ways. While the latter is concerned largely with how national news media can promote democracy and good governance, the former prioritizes the role of IKCS in improving local livelihoods and local development. The community development strand also aims to strengthen traditional governance systems – based on trust, personal relationships, networks and social capital – rather than promoting governance in terms of national elections and policy-making (ibid.: 125). Manyozo describes the community development strand as being characterized by a focus on self-management and sustainability rather than dependence on donor and government funding. Thus, by promoting community engagement and empowerment, community media may perform a very different kind of role in media development.

But while community media may lend themselves to promoting a different form of media development to the good governance strand, community media practices around the world are also extremely varied. Given this, it is helpful to consider a fourfold typology for interpreting the various roles that different forms of community media can play in development (see Bailey et al. 2007; Carpentier et al. 2008). The most conventional view of community media is as forms of media designed to serve a community. A community can be defined geographically, but also by a shared ethnicity, common interest or broader sense of belonging. Saint FM, for example, is a community radio station based on the island of St Helena in the South Atlantic Ocean. It aims to maintain a sense of common identity and belonging, not only for the geographically defined community of those living on the island, but also for those islanders who have moved to other countries. Community radio stations based in internally displaced peoples (IDP) camps also rely upon a broad definition of community – and may even play a role in the construction of the community. In this approach, emphasis is placed on the participation of the community in the production and reception of media content and its value lies in the capacity to validate the community and empower those who participate.

Secondly, Nico Carpentier, Rico Lie and Jan Serveas (2008) suggest that community media can be defined in opposition to mainstream media. Such *alternative* media might define themselves through being oriented towards specific audiences, rather than a mass market, by being independent from state or corporate control and/or by having a horizontal, rather than a vertical, management structure. Most commonly, though, alternative media are defined through their content – by focusing on the communication of counter-hegemonic discourses. In their account of this typology, Olga Bailey, Bart Cammaerts and Nico Carpentier (2007) cite various examples of blogging during the second Iraq War – including by Iraqi citizens, US military personnel and in photo-blogs – as examples of alternative media generating content that runs counter to mainstream media discourses.

A third perspective on community media emphasizes their role as part of civil society, or as a 'third voice' between state media and private commercial media (rather than an alternative or minority voice). In this context, community media help to expand and deepen democracy by increasing the number and range of voices participating in public debate (Carpentier et al. 2008). An example of community radio serving this function is Radio Ada, Ghana's first community radio station, which has a long-standing reputation for targeting and encouraging the participation of marginalized community members. Between 2008 and 2013 it was involved in the Mwananchi Project, which was designed to reduce communal tensions around the governance of important local salt resources by facilitating more inclusive discussion of the issue by all community members. It focused particularly on the inclusion of migrants, women, children and the disabled, for whom salt is one of the few options for revenue generation available. Radio Ada also sought to generate demand for a stronger commitment to accountability, transparency and inclusiveness of the trusteeship of the local salt-producing lagoon. In doing so, Radio Ada amplified the voice of the local community and its participation in local decision-making processes.

Finally, community media can be conceived of as 'rhizomatic' – or as non-linear, anarchic and nomadic. In this approach, their key defining feature is their elusiveness and contingency (ibid.: 359). The significance of community media here lies in their potential catalysing role – in their ability to connect different aspects of civil society, such as women's, peasants' and students' movements, with each other or with different segments of the state and the market, without them losing their proper identity. Bailey et al. (2007: 47) use the example of the Brazilian film *Radio Favela* to illustrate the function of rhizomatic community media. *Radio Favela* is based on the true story of how a group of four friends from the *favelas* of Belo Horizonte set up their own pirate radio station in the 1980s. Throughout the film there are instances which demonstrate how the station is intimately connected, in complex (rhizomatic) ways, with multiple other institutions, including other organizations in the *favela*, political parties and advertisers, but also with the broader political struggle in Brazil at the time. The example of *Radio Favela* is also used to demonstrate that these four perspectives on community media are not mutually exclusive – they can both coexist and overlap within an organization (ibid.).

In summary, it should be clear that there are many different forms of community media which have multiple, complex and often overlapping roles in relation to development. While the functions of community-based media may not always fall neatly into the good governance strand of media development which dominates the field, it should also be clear that they cannot be ignored in any effort to fully understand the social, political and economic functions of the media in society.

Conclusion

Despite the critical approach of this chapter, to be clear, the main argument here has not been that media development does not matter for development. Far from it. I have outlined various ways in which media development is likely to be very important for democratization, good governance, economic development and many other interpretations of development. Instead, the main aim of this chapter has been to highlight that links between development and media development are multiple, complex and contingent. As Amelia Arsenault and Shawn Powers (2010: 31) put it, 'there is no agreement about when, how, and under what conditions media development can or should be practiced'.

Unfortunately, the lack of clear lines of causality between media development and development makes it very difficult to demonstrate the importance of supporting the media. As Thomas Huyghebaert from the European Commission put it (cited in Alcorn et al. 2011: 11), 'media development is not about building roads. We can't measure the impact of our projects by measuring the number of roads built. We need to understand the difficulty of determining appropriate indicators.' Anne Nelson (cited in ibid.: 11) goes farther, arguing that 'the inputs and the outputs of media development monitoring and evaluation often don't make sense ... They are pretending causality in situations that have multi-causal relationships.'

One organization that has taken this argument to heart is Panos South Asia, which, in a publication entitled *Spheres of Influence* (Panneerselvan and Nair 2008: 8, 10), rather bravely admitted that

> There is broad consensus that ... [the Panos Network] do
> not expect to directly bring about measurable change at the
> grassroots level ... The need of the hour is to scale down
> expectations given the truth that the impact of media related
> programmes take[s] well beyond project completion to per-
> colate and manifest. No amount of number crunching will
> lead to direct correlation between cause and effect attribution.
> The goal post needs to be realigned with media development
> organisations accepting humbly that they can only be co-
> contributors to an effect.

Indeed, the underlying proposition in this chapter, and in this book overall, is that while there are numerous ways in which the media matter for development, it is not helpful to emphasize only the potentially positive consequences. By providing a critical introduction to, in this case, the field of media development, I hope to simultaneously draw attention to the role of media in development, and at the same time to do so in a manner that highlights the complexity and contingency of the media's role.

5 | Strategies of Humanitarian Communication: Choose Wisely

This chapter introduces the topic of media representations of development, which is concerned with the causes, content and consequences of media representations of development and of the global South, as they are communicated to audiences in the global North. In particular, the chapter critically examines three dominant forms of humanitarian communication used by non-governmental organizations (NGOs) in the global North – 'shock effect' appeals, deliberate positivism and post-humanitarian communication. Throughout, the focus is on defining and critiquing these different strategies of NGO communications, both on their own terms and from a more critical perspective. The recurring criticisms of these styles of campaigning centre on: how the need for NGO work is justified, what forms of action audiences are invited to take, and whether NGO communications reinforce or challenge discourses of global inequality. The chapter also discusses the potential implications of new technologies for humanitarian communication.

The central argument in this chapter is that there is no ideal form of humanitarian communication, only a series of similarly problematic compromises in response to the intractable and often irresolvable tensions inherent within NGO communications. This is not to say that some practices are not preferable to others. Humanitarian communications should always seek to maximize the potential for dignity, understanding, proximity and effective action. Rather, the point is that humanitarian communications are affected by broader tensions which can never be fully reconciled. These include the inherent difficulty of taking effective action to address faraway suffering, the challenge of avoiding reproducing hierarchies of human life when this is at the heart of NGOs' work, and the inescapable influence of broader political and commercial drivers of NGO appeals.

This argument contributes to the wider aims of this book by demonstrating that although strategies of humanitarian communication are important – for raising funds, legitimizing the work of NGOs or for reinforcing discourses of global inequality – this does not justify a naive celebration of their influence. Ultimately, strategies of humanitarian communication are themselves shaped by the political, economic and sociocultural context in which they are produced. Media may matter for development, but only in concert with many other different factors.

In order to make this argument clear, it is useful to conceive of alternative strategies of humanitarian communication, not as offering better or worse representations of distant suffering, but as adopting different approaches to mediation. Mediation here is defined as a 'dialectical and institutionally and technologically driven phenomenon' (Silverstone 2006: 189) that involves both 'overcoming distance in communication' (Tomlinson 1999: 154) and the process of 'passing through the medium' (ibid.: 155). It is preferred to the notion of 'representations' here because it does a better job of capturing the complex ways in which media are implicated in the relationship between audiences and distant suffering, beyond making images and narratives available. It suggests that media affect the ways in which individuals experience space and time and therefore that they can bring distant suffering closer to audiences, while at the same time recognizing that the presence of the medium interferes with this process.

It is also useful to distinguish between two coexisting,

mutually dependent dimensions of mediation – those of immediacy and hypermediacy. Immediacy is defined as 'a style of visual representation whose goal is to make the viewer forget the presence of the medium and believe that he [or she] is in the presence of the objects of representation' (Bolter and Grusin 2000: 272). This is the dimension of mediation which allows for the images and scenes audiences witness to act upon their emotions as if what they were watching were real. As such, it draws our attention to the process of overcoming distance in communication. Yet media do not simply bring things closer to us. Immediacy cannot exist without hypermediacy, or the process of passing through the medium. Hypermediacy is defined by Jay Bolter and Richard Grusin (ibid.: 272) as 'a style of visual representation whose goal is to remind the viewer of the medium'. It is this dimension of mediation which allows audiences to recognize that the experiences we have when consuming media are brought about through the presence of a medium, such as through the on-screen ribbons of text, photographs and graphics on twenty-four-hour news channels.

These concepts of mediation, immediacy and hypermediacy help us to move away from imprecise and normative judgement about positive or negative strategies and instead suggest that all forms of humanitarian communication are essentially different ways of attempting to overcome the distance between audiences and faraway others through various strategies of mediation (or combinations of immediacy and hypermediacy).

'Shock effect' appeals

Defining 'negative' campaigns The most constructive place to begin a critical review of humanitarian communications is with the notorious practice of 'shock effect' (Benthall 2010) appeals. Looking beyond the largely imprecise and normative accounts of this term in the literature, perhaps the most useful definition is given by John Cameron and Anna Haanstra (2008: 1476). They describe shock effect appeals as NGO campaigns which 'aim to provoke feelings of guilt and pity in Western audiences through portrayals of extreme material poverty and suffering'. The most frequently cited examples of this come from the campaigns associated with the famine in Ethiopia in 1983–85 and the subsequent Live Aid concerts (see Franks 2014). But shock effect imagery is certainly not a purely historical phenomenon. Nandita Dogra's (2012: 64) analysis of NGO advertisements in UK newspapers from 2005 to 2006 shows that shock effect campaigns still 'form a substantial proportion of INGOs' messages' today. They appear in the form of daytime television advertisements run by Save the Children and often in campaigns associated with humanitarian crises, such as the 2011 East Africa famine and the Syrian refugee crisis.

From Cameron and Haanstra's definition, we can identify the first key feature of shock effect campaigns as being their attempts to document the apparent 'plain reality', or 'raw realism' (Chouliaraki 2011: 110), of suffering. The role of the medium in these campaigns is to provide evidence as compelling as possible of the physical condition of suffering, so that audiences cannot deny its existence. In other words, shock effect campaigns focus on immediacy rather than hypermediacy. Such attempts to overcome the distance between audiences and distant suffering through confronting audiences with the 'bare life' (Agamben 1998) of faraway strangers are often achieved through a fetishizing of the body. The camera focuses, close up, on naked or semi-naked bodies to provide graphic evidence of malnourishment, for example. As Machiel Lamers (2005: 47) concludes from a study of Belgian NGOs' fund-raising posters, 'in some cases it is only the children's eyes that are portrayed, the face or just a hand'. It is this fetishizing of the body which has prompted comparisons with pornography. Just as sexual pornography involves exposure of the body, so shock effect appeals involve the exposing of the raw reality of life – or a pornography of poverty. As Jørgen Lissner (1981: 23) put it, 'it exposes something in human life that is as delicate and deeply personal as sexuality, that is, suffering'.

Despite attempting to act as a faithful testimony to the genuineness of suffering by documenting its raw reality, shock effect approaches are not intended to act upon audiences' rational faculties (Cohen 2001: 183). Rather, as Cameron and Haanstra suggest, they act upon the specific emotional responses of pity and guilt. Pity is a response to the witnessing of the spectacle of many people suffering through no apparent fault of their own (Boltanski 1999: 1–5) and is generated through the focus on raw reality. The evocation of a sense of guilt is a little more complex. It derives from what Lilie Chouliaraki (2010: 111) describes as the 'logic of complicity', whereby our failure to act, despite our being a witness to the horrors of suffering, leaves us in some way complicit in the suffering of distant others. As Thomas Haskell (1985) argues, while we may not be invited to regard ourselves as the direct cause of suffering, if we recognize that our refusal to act when confronted with distant suffering is a necessary condition for the suffering to persist, then we still remain, to some extent, causally involved. We can no longer say we didn't know, and now that we know, if we are not part of the solution, we are, in effect, part of the problem. In order to alleviate the resulting feeling of guilt we are compelled to take action, most often in the form of charitable giving. The simpler the action – *Buy (Red), Save lives* – the more guilty you should feel if you still do not take it (Cohen 2001: 182).

Another feature of humanitarian communications in the form of shock effect appeals is that they rely, not simply on the representation of victims, but on the construction of sufferers as 'ideal victims' (Höijer 2004). Discourses of global compassion circulated by media and implied by international politics designate some victims as more worthy, or deserving of our pity, than others. According to Edward Herman and Noam Chomsky (1988: 38), for example, people abused in what are regarded as enemy states are routinely portrayed in the media 'as worthy victims, whereas those treated with equal or greater severity by ... [their] own government or clients will be unworthy'. Thus, in order for humanitarian communications to attempt to generate the strongest response, victims must be seen as both innocent and as helpless (Höijer 2004). If victims are understood to be somehow culpable in their own suffering or responsible for the suffering of others, then they are unlikely to generate pity. Similarly, if victims are able to act in some way to relieve their own suffering, then this may diminish the perceived need for external assistance. As Susan Moeller (1999: 107) puts it, 'only when victims have been identified as "bona fide" are they candidates for compassion'.

This requirement for innocence and helplessness explains the frequent focus on children in shock effect imagery. As Lamers (2005: 47) explains, 'everybody understands that you need to protect a child and take care of a child because of its vulnerability and innocence'. Specifically, images of powerless children appeal to 'parenting instincts of care and protection' (Manzo 2008: 650) and generate pity 'through our own memory of being open and vulnerable to the treachery of adulthood' (Höijer 2004: 522). In his study of Belgian NGO poster campaigns, Lamers (2005) finds that the most frequently appearing images over the last thirty-five years were of a child – appearing in around 50 per cent of posters. Indeed, a focus on children is often central to many definitions of shock effect imagery. Betty Plewes and Rieky Stuart (2007: 23), for example, define this style of campaigning as 'images of emaciated children with distended bellies or flies in their eyes'.

Bound up with this requirement for ideal victims is a further feature of shock effect approaches. These styles of campaigns are utterly victim centred, in that the focus is entirely on the condition of the sufferer rather than the cause or explanations of the suffering. Put another way, in shock effect approaches, documenting the reality of suffering is given precedence over attempts to explain the complex, longer-term, structural causes of suffering. As Stan Cohen (2001: 183) wrote, 'these photos lack context – just the face, neck and shoulders of a crying "ethnic" child'. Chouliaraki (2006: 99) describes this as the presentation of a 'logic of appearances' in which causality is presented as being dictated by the immediate context rather than historical circumstances, as opposed to a 'logic of causality' in which the longer-term consequences and more subtle contexts are revealed. At its most extreme, a logic of appearances presents events as naturalized, or simply as 'the kind of thing that happens over there' (Cohen 2001: 177).

This logic of appearances and focus on the victim are part of a wider 'humanitarian narrative' (Benthall 2010) that shock effect campaigns conform to, which depicts helpless victims being confronted by localized problems to which only the aid organization in question can respond (Kennedy 2009). As Cohen (2001: 174) explains, 'stories of social suffering have become stories of humanitarian intervention'. This narrative is necessary for creating a clear and direct link between accounts of what is happening, why it is happening and what we can do about it – thereby providing a simple and direct reason for giving money (Lamers 2005: 51). The assumption here is that introducing complexities can provide alibis for passivity by inviting audiences to feel that their monetary contribution may not directly contribute to improving the situation.

The price of shock effect campaigns There are a number of well-established criticisms levelled at shock effect campaigns. The first criticism is made on moral grounds and contends that such images deprive the sufferers depicted, and the many more individuals they are used to represent, of their dignity. Plewes and Stuart (2007: 23), for example, describe these campaigns as 'the worst images that exploit the poor for little more than voyeuristic ends and where people are portrayed as helpless, passive objects'. This criticism is often linked to the claim that these campaigns are unrepresentative or that they provide a distortion of reality. As Mark Goldring (cited in VSO 2001: 3) argues, 'if the media portrayal of the developing world is understood to be so distorted that it deceives audiences about their true position in the world then we have a moral duty to reform it'.

There is a tension here, however, because while these campaigns may be interpreted as lacking 'respect for people's dignity and privacy', or as being 'misleading by omission' (Plewes and Stuart 2007: 34), representativeness is a problematic criterion by which to judge NGO communications. As Robert Martin (1994: 186) argues, 'parts of Africa are places of famine and disease and not to report on such topics would itself be a distortion'. Cohen (2001: 183–4) extends this argument further when he asks,

> why demand that they are an accurate statistical sample?
> Surely the point is to represent the problem at its worst ... If
> the[y] had to think each time about representativeness rather
> than representation, this would undermine, not to say miss the
> whole point of – their work ... I believe that unless 'negative
> imagery' is allowed to speak for itself, the universality of suf-
> fering will never be acknowledged.

Moreover, there is a consensus in the NGO sector, born out of extensive experience and research, that shock effect campaigns are still the most effective at raising funds, particularly for urgent humanitarian appeals. This is the main reason why NGOs continue to use them. Thus, while such campaigns may raise important ethical issues, they also raise more money than any other style of campaign, thereby allowing NGOs to perform their work. The defence of this approach, therefore, is that the financial benefits outweigh the ethical considerations.

The main challenge to this particular argument is that although shock effect campaigns may be effective at fund-raising in the short term, they have more damaging long-term implications both for public awareness and fund-raising efforts. The notion of compassion fatigue is used in this context to refer to the perceived general sense of audience apathy towards the wider world in which the public are subsequently less inclined to engage in overseas giving as a result of the repeated use of the same disaster narratives in the media (Moeller 1999: 3). In their empirical research into the compassion fatigue thesis, Katherine Kinnick and her colleagues (1996) find evidence that this apparent indifference to global suffering is the result of the tendency of the media to present problems but not their solutions, an emphasis on the sensational and a lack of context. Contributing to this sense of compassion fatigue is a seemingly well-entrenched tendency for audiences to resist campaigns which are designed to make them feel guilt or pity. Chouliaraki (2011: 112) refers to this as 'the boomerang effect' or people's resistance to the negativity of campaigns themselves.

It is important to note that while publics in the global North (and South) may indeed have a general resistance to shock effect NGO campaigns, the concept of compassion fatigue itself has been widely criticized for being 'over-used, vague as a description and even vaguer as an explanation' (Cohen 2001: 191). It lacks clarity as a way of describing public dispositions towards distant others, it is used to mean different things in different situations, and operates via different causal chains accordingly. The real problem, Cohen (ibid.: 192) suggests, is 'the media's framework of reporting, rather than the public's capacity to keep absorbing'.

From a more critical perspective, shock effect campaigns are accused of reinforcing a hierarchy of human life between the lives of those in front of the television screens and those suffering on them (Chouliaraki 2006: 4). Notions of Northern supremacy are reinforced through the reproduction of the idea that 'benevolent donors in the North are the primary source of solutions for the "problems" of the South' (Cameron and Haanstra 2008: 1478). The inferiority of the global South is maintained by the myth of their powerlessness, or inability to help themselves. These colonial visions are compounded by the iconography of childhood (Manzo 2008: 636), whereby pictures of children symbolize the weak, vulnerable and dependent position that developing countries have in relation to the stronger, richer and more dominant developed countries (Lamers 2005: 49).

Indeed, in a survey of 1,000 UK adults in 2001, 74 per cent stated that they believed developing countries 'depend on the money and knowledge of the West to progress' (VSO 2001: 3). The qualitative findings of the same research provided evidence that the British public had a strong sense of superiority over developing countries, which they regarded as helpless victims and grateful receivers of Western aid. The authors concluded that these 'stereotypical beliefs and outdated images hold a vice-like grip on British understanding of the developing world' and that this is, to a significant extent, a legacy of 'live aid'.

This naturalizing of the power relations between the West and the 'rest' is important because it promotes a development agenda that is deeply anti-political, or what Jan Nederveen Pieterse (1995: 235) refers to as an 'aid assistance imagination'. Following this argument, Cameron and Haanstra (2008: 1478) describe these campaigns as reinforcing the 'strong cultural grounding in the North for paternalistic, charity-based and frequently neo-colonial development practices and projects'. The tendency to focus on 'victims' rather than the causes of suffering masks the need for a commitment to long-term structural change and conceals the complicity of actors in the North in shaping poverty and global inequality (Lissner 1977: 238). As Pieterse (1995: 235) puts it,

> The question of how Africa, once a producer of food surpluses, ended up in its present condition is rarely addressed … The role of colonialism, the consequences of export agriculture and the effects of the agricultural and trade policies of western countries are issues that remain outside the framework of the advertisements of western charity.

In summary, shock effect appeals can be defined as a strategy of humanitarian communication which focuses on the raw reality of the suffering of worthy victims in order to convey a situation that is 'urgent, open to remedy and "real"' (Radley and Kennedy 1997: 438) and provokes feelings of guilt and pity. While it may be seemingly effective at raising money for NGOs in the short term, it also has significant implications for global power relations, ethics and longer-term efforts at building a constituency of support for development (Edwards 1999). It also has a role to play in reinforcing a negative self-image of the people being portrayed and for migrants and diaspora communities. It is in response to such criticisms that many alternative forms of humanitarian communication have arisen. But as we shall see, they may not actually resolve the problems discussed here, only revise them.

Deliberate positivism

Defining 'positive' campaigns Shock effect approaches were the dominant form of humanitarian communication in many countries in Europe and North America up until the mid-1980s. However, in response to the criticisms discussed above there was a distinct shift in the late 1980s and beyond towards the use of 'positive image' appeals, often referred to as 'deliberate positivism' (Lidchi 1999). Deliberate positivism refers to humanitarian communications which focus on providing evidence of the direct, positive, effects that the actions of donors have allegedly had on beneficiaries. As one Plan International advertisement reads, 'Sponsor a child with Plan. See the difference.' Such imagery is more of a feature of regular fund-raising rather than emergency appeals, and takes the form, most often, of photos of smiling children, as in Christian Aid, UNICEF or Save the Children leaflets, for example. It is also evident in the personal stories of World Vision child sponsors and the 'success stories' of Concern's latest project.

In a similar way to shock effect approaches, the role of the medium in deliberate positivism is to provide evidence of the reality of the lives of development partners. In other words, it also preferences immediacy over hypermediacy. But unlike shock effect approaches, in deliberate positivism the testimony provided by the medium is used to reflect the individuality, dignity and agency of individuals. Subjects are personalized by being named, being given a voice, or by being depicted in situations which may confound existing stereotypes. This personalization presents individuals as possessing a greater degree of agency and of being more humanized, or like 'us'. This is significant because it invites the audience to acknowledge, to some extent, the sense of shared humanity between themselves and the subject. Thus, the appeal for audiences to act within these campaigns is based, partly, on a sense of empathy, or feeling for fellow human beings who are, or were, suffering (Chouliaraki 2013).

In deliberate positivism this individualization and corresponding appeal to empathy is combined with an attempt to demonstrate that the donor is able 'to make a concrete contribution to improve a sufferer's life' (Chouliaraki 2010: 112). The role of the text is to provide evidence for the audience that their actions can lead to positive and demonstrable change. In this way, it directly challenges the sense of compassion fatigue, or powerlessness, seemingly generated by the repeated use of shock effect appeals. The particular emotion by which this appeal to act operates is gratitude. A smiling face, for example, connotates, not only that circumstances have been improved, but also a sense of the relief of being having 'saved' (Manzo 2008: 640). In so doing, it provides subtle evidence of gratitude for the alleviation of suffering by a benefactor (Chouliaraki 2010: 113). In summary, whereas shock effect approaches work through activating feelings of guilt and pity, positive images work through activating emotions of gratitude and empathy.

Positive image approaches also differ from shock effect campaigns because of their tendency to focus on longer-term development issues rather than short-term aid and humanitarian relief. This makes deliberate positivism particularly attractive for NGOs in some contexts because it better reflects and supports an ideology of development interventions based on challenging longer-term causes of poverty and inequality. One of the lessons learnt from the intense debates about humanitarian communication in the 1980s was that there is an important link between strategies of representation and NGO practices (Lidchi 1999: 95; Dogra 2007). As is stated in the 1989 European NGO Code of Conduct on Images and Messages Relating to the Third World, 'the problem of images and perceptions cannot be separated from the methodology of intervention'. Indeed, NGO appeal strategies play a role, not just in fund-raising or public awareness, but in providing legitimacy and political leverage for NGOs. Choosing positive images over shock effect appeals can be as much a statement about the brand, politics or ideology of the NGO, as an attempt to raise funds (Cottle and Nolan 2007).

Deliberate positivism and shock effects: two sides of the same coin? Despite their apparent differences, though, there is much that unites positive image and shock effect approaches. Both rely on generating a sense of realism in order to produce appeals for action. While there is often an assumption that positive images are more representative of the true lives of development partners, because they attempt to reflect their dignity and self-determination, their evidence of truth is no more complete than in shock effect approaches. Such campaigns have been accused of focusing only on the small-scale, short-term, positive effects of fund-raising and of glossing over the very real miseries and intractability of suffering (Benthall 2010: 186). Similarly, such campaigns often reproduce stereotypes of an idyllic agrarian 'Third World', populated only by farmers on their smallholdings (Dogra 2007: 170). Plewes and Stuart (2007: 29), for example, describe a collection of such campaign material as consisting mostly of depictions of 'rural life and primary producers with few pictures of urban areas, industrial production, artistic expression, or cultural life. There was almost no sense of context.'

Moreover, despite its focus on longer-term development issues, the strategy of deliberate positivism still conceals crucial aspects of the complexity of development, just as shock effect images do. Chouliaraki (2010: 113) accuses them of failing to

Critically address the hegemony of neoliberal politics in world economy, the competitive governance milieu in which NGOs operate, the conditions of marketization and mediatization on which their legitimacy rests, the problematic links between NGOs and local regimes, as well as the lack of local infrastructures often leading to failures of development. In suppressing these complex dimensions of development, 'positive' appeals seem to lack a certain reflexivity as to the limits of the interventionist project to promote sustainable social change.

Furthermore, while deliberate positivism appears to empower through discourses of dignity and agency, the continued reliance on charitable donations as a means of action ensures that 'they' remain objects of 'our' generosity (Chouliaraki 2013: 63). Charitable Northern interventions are still the only way to create happiness in the South. This reinforcing of asymmetries of power between North and South is compounded by a reliance on gratitude, which sustains a clear hierarchy of human life between the grateful receiver and the benevolent donor.

Finally, while deliberate positivism may set out to combat the sense of compassion fatigue generated by shock effect approaches, it too has been accused of fostering resistance to action – in this case by promoting the idea that help isn't needed. By providing evidence of the apparent progress achieved as a result of development assistance, deliberate positivism runs the risk of presenting the problems as having been fully addressed, thus leading to inaction on the grounds that 'everything is already taken care of' (ibid.: 63). Put simply, 'if people are portrayed as *not* asking for your help, why then should you offer this help?' (Cohen 2001: 180).

In her review of deliberate positivism Nandita Dogra (2007: 168) concludes by asking whether 'it is just the safest way out of the criticisms of "negative" imagery?' Although it might appear to be a safer option than shock effect images, there is, as Cohen (2001: 180) puts it, 'little ideological variation between the resulting texts'. They both conceal the complexities of development, reproduce hierarchies of human life and potentially foster resistance to action. Perhaps it is more helpful to describe the strategies of deliberate positivism and shock effects as part of a 'realist impasse' (Lidchi 1999: 101) in humanitarian communication, in which NGOs are reliant upon images which claim to document reality. This reliance on mediation as immediacy is based on a faith in the power of knowledge, or the idea that if only people knew, if they were confronted with sufficient evidence of suffering, they would act (Cohen 2001: 185). Given the apparent failure of both forms of humanitarian communication to generate sustained, large-scale public action vis-à-vis distant suffering, it appears that such assumptions about the power of knowing may be somewhat misguided. Luc Boltanski (1999: xvi) refers to this as the 'crisis of pity'. In response, a new form of *post*-humanitarian communication has emerged, which appears to overcome this realist impasse.

Post-humanitarian communication

Chouliaraki (2013) uses the term *post*-humanitarian to define campaigns which break with both the aesthetic conventions and the moral mechanisms of conventional humanitarian appeals (such as shock effect campaigns and positive imagery). In post-humanitarian communication, public action towards distant suffering is based on 'low intensity emotional regimes' (Chouliaraki 2010: 119), or regimes of emotion towards suffering which do not quite inspire or enact grand emotions such as guilt and pity, or empathy and gratitude. These 'low-intensity emotional regimes' appear, not as immediate emotions that may inspire action, but as objects of contemplation to be reflected upon (ibid.: 118). For example, a campaign may invite audiences to engage in self-reflection about food waste in the West and the chronic shortage of food elsewhere in the world, or invite us to contemplate the consequences of our indifference towards distant suffering. The focus of any emotional response here is primarily on the self rather than on the suffering other, who is often entirely absent from the campaign. This focus on the self in post-humanitarian communications is made explicit in campaign slogans such as 'she can change your life forever' (Plan International advertisement, 1993) and the We Can be Heroes campaign, which uses the slogan 'in a time of crisis, one small act can make you a hero'.

The second key feature of the moral mechanism through which post-humanitarian communication works is simplicity. This refers to the requirement for relatively undemanding actions in response to suffering, often online, such as signing an on-line petition, clicking a 'donate' button or following a link to an NGO website. Such immediate, on-the-spot, actions allow for 'instant gratification' in response to suffering as they do not require a commitment to a cause for any length of time (Chouliaraki 2013: 70). The major requirement for taking part in Oxfam's 2013 Food for All campaign, for example, was to 'spread the word' by picking and sharing your favourite Food for All photos from the Oxfam Facebook album.

This simplicity also refers to the lack of apparent justification in the appeals. Whereas shock effect appeals and deliberate positivism both draw on universal discourses of ethics (and consequently risk evoking a sense of compassion fatigue), post-humanitarian communication abandons attempts to tell audiences how they should feel when confronted with suffering. Indeed, suffering others are themselves often entirely absent from such campaigns. Instead, they rely on the reputation and image of the organizational brand itself to signal the nature and value of the cause. For example, the Digital Death campaign, launched on World AIDS day 2010, involved the world's most followed celebrity Tweeters – including Alicia Keys, Lady Gaga, Justin Timberlake and Serena Williams – refusing to post any more Twitter or Facebook updates until US$1 million was donated to the charity Keep a Child Alive. The campaign focused almost entirely on the digital 'death' of the celebrities – including images of celebrities posed in coffins – rather than on the lives of the people the money was directed at helping. Moreover, the primary justification for acting upon suffering was provided by the Keep a Child Alive brand and the celebrities' sacrifice, rather than a detailed account of the importance of tackling HIV/AIDS in Africa and India. The digital lives of all the celebrities were 'bought back' in just six days.

In order to achieve this break from appeals to grand emotions, characteristic of conventional humanitarian communications, post-humanitarian communication adopts alternative aesthetic conventions. Rather than attempt to document the reality of distant suffering, post-humanitarian communication relies on what Plewes and Stuart (2007: 32) describe as 'clever or ironic images'. Examples of such 'playful textualities' or 'textual games' (Chouliaraki 2010) include abstract art or graphic animations, as used in Oxfam's 2008 'Be Humankind' appeal, or the juxta-position of space and time, as in Amnesty International's 'It is not happening here but now' campaigns in 2006. In Bolter and Grusin's terminology, we would say that post-humanitarian communication favours hypermediacy over immediacy because of its reliance on various combinations of image, sound, text, animation and video, which draw attention to the act of seeing itself. The intention of such practices is to challenge attempts to present the truth of suffering, from which compassion fatigue de-rives, and instead to draw attention to the problem of accurately representing suffering as itself a part of their appeal to act upon it (Chouliaraki 2010: 373). In other words, post-humanitarian communication deliberately draws attention to the presence of the medium (hypermediacy), rather than trying to mask its existence (immediacy). In so doing, it invites audiences to engage, not in grand emotions, but in 'reflexive particularism' (ibid.: 120), or to rely on our own judgement as to whether public action is possible or desirable in any particular instance.

In summary, post-humanitarian communication is characterized by a reliance on textual games rather than on realism and by a corresponding appeal to 'low intensity emotional regimes' and short-term forms of agency, rather than grand emotions and sustained commitment. The strength of post-humanitarian communication lies, not necessarily in its ability to raise money, but in its relevance in an increasingly defragmented, commercialized and competitive media environment. This may make it well suited to achieving alternative objectives such as brand differentiation, retaining or reaching specific audiences, advocacy or influencing international policy arenas.

Chouliaraki (ibid.) argues that the emergence of post-humanitarian communication is a logical response to the compassion fatigue seemingly generated by conventional humanitarian campaigns. By relying on appeals to a universal morality and by seeking to activate grand emotions through realist representational practices, conventional humanitarian campaigns fail to recognize our inherent inability to act on all instances of distant suffering. In response to this, post-humanitarian communication not only accepts the problems inherent in acting at a distance but defines itself through the explicit articulation of this issue. But it may also have gone too far in this direction; by inviting audiences to engage in simple actions, as and when they see fit, does post-humanitarian communication ask too little of the public? Will it not fail to inspire sustained commitment to moral causes?

Furthermore, in post-humanitarian communication, solidarity with the suffering is grounded, not on a direct engagement with the distant others and with a complex understanding of their circumstances, but on self-reflection. Are we comfortable that our personal preference for one cause over another is driven, not on a sound understanding of the complex causes of others' plight, but on the relative effectiveness of the branding strategy of different campaigns? Is it right that the principal motivation to act should be a personal project of moral self-fulfilment; to make ourselves better people?

Moreover, while post-humanitarian campaigns may have emerged in response to the compassion fatigue generated by traditional iconographies of suffering, at least such campaigns enabled audiences to encounter suffering others. The absence, or 'annihilation' (Silverstone 2002a), of others in post-humanitarian campaigns arguably reproduces an even more extreme inequality of human life by dehumanizing distant others to the point of non-existence. As Choukliaraki (2011: 372) puts it, 'Instead of enabling us to hear their voice and get an insight into their lives, it treats distant others as voiceless props that evoke responses of self-expression, but cannot in themselves become anything more than shadow figures in someone else's story.'

Thus, while post-humanitarian communication may have emerged in response to the apparent failures of conventional NGO campaigns, it appears to suffer, perhaps even more acutely, from some of the same issues, such as reproducing unequal power relations and failing to educate or inspire sustained commitment from audiences. Put another way, strategies of humanitarian communication based on hypermediacy are no less problematic than those based on immediacy.

Humanitarian communication online

The internet and web 2.0 technologies certainly offer NGOs a greater range of tools for use in their campaigns. But do they have the capacity to address the problems associated with the various forms of NGO communication discussed above? If the use of these technologies is subject to the same pressures and constraints as conventional mass-media campaigns, won't the strategies (and problems) of shock effects, deliberate positivism and post-humanitarian communication simply shift online? This final section considers how new technologies may, or may not, help to provide more context, allow for different and more varied forms of action, and challenge hierarchies of human life. In doing so it also helps identify some of the key tensions inherent in humanitarian communication, regardless of what technologies are used.

New technologies and the complexities of development One of the key issues in NGO campaigns, of all forms, is the tendency to simplify development issues. In shock effect approaches, the causes of famine, for example, are related simply to a lack of food supply, rather than access. In deliberate positivism, the actions of donors are constructed as automatically having a direct, positive, predictable and demonstrable effect on beneficiaries. In post-humanitarian communication, the justification of action is tied only to brand recognition. Moreover, the traditional technologies used to communicate these campaigns can be accused of compounding such simplifications. The latest Code of Conduct on Images and Messages of the General Assembly of European NGOs (CONCORD 2006) suggests that NGOs should seek to represent a 'complete picture' of development. But is this really possible? As Cohen (2001: 182) puts it, 'yes, the subject is far too complex to be reduced to an image of a child. But what photo would convey the complex causes of poverty in Bangladesh – a board meeting of the IMF?'

In this context, web technologies might appear to offer the opportunity for more complex, nuanced and multidimensional portrayals of the global South. Indeed, a recent report specifically addressing this issue concluded that 'traditional media provides audiences with the "bigger picture", but the internet is better suited to answering specific questions and providing personal points of connection with people and issues' (Fenyoe 2010: 12). As Denis Kennedy (2009: 1) argues, the internet 'can help us better visualise and know a place: articles can be backed with links, stories can be supplemented with refugee narratives, a full array of photos can be used'.

But despite providing a number of *opportunities* for revealing the complexities of development, the political and commercial environment in which such campaigns take place, which affect the justifications and explanations provided by NGO campaigns, remains unaffected by a shift online. It is generally not in the interests of NGOs to reveal the difficulties and compromises of development work to their supporters, whether their campaigns are online or offline, because complex explanations are always likely to inhibit charitable donations. Equally, in contemporary information societies where there is fierce competition for audience attention, humanitarian communications almost inevitably need to omit detail in order to grab attention quickly and be clear in their messaging. In short, while new media may offer NGOs the opportunity to provide more complex accounts of poverty and development, they do not affect the drivers which influence their willingness to do so (Smith 2011).

Online action Another major issue with the use of traditional media technologies in NGO campaigns is that they do not afford the opportunity of immediate action. As Boltanski (1999: xv) puts it,

> When confronted with suffering, all moral demands converge on the single imperative of action ... But what form can this

commitment [to action] take when those called upon to act are thousands of miles away from the person suffering, comfortably installed in front of the television set in the shelter of the family living room?

Furthermore, the form of action most often demanded in conventional humanitarian communication is charitable giving, which, as has been argued, reinforces a particular humanitarian narrative in which only Northern charity can resolve problems in the South.

In this context, Kennedy (2009: 1) argues that new technologies '[supply] us with new ways of acting at a distance and new ways of influencing future events ... Our feelings of moral obligation can stay the same; all that changes is an expansion of the range of opportunities available to us.' This range of opportunities includes signing online petitions, making instant ethical purchases, sharing information, recruiting volunteers and organizing offline campaign activities. In June 2011 Greenpeace launched an online campaign aimed at persuading the toy manufacturer Mattel to stop using products from Asia Pulp and Paper (APP), a company allegedly involved in destroying Indonesian rainforests. This campaign centred on an online spoof video of Ken breaking up with Barbie because of her environmentally damaging packaging. The weight of public response to the campaign, generated through social media, contributed to an announcement by Mattel in October 2011 that it was adopting a new paper-buying policy and new sustainable sourcing principles. Other high-profile examples of NGOs making use of the opportunities for public action provided by new media include One Billion Rising, the IF campaign and the heavily criticized Kony 2012 (see Chalk 2012).

However, taking action online brings with it its own set of issues. Making it ever easier for users to participate in campaigns, albeit in a range of different ways, may promote nothing more than the illusion of involvement. Suggesting that a few non-committal, low-effort, mouse clicks is all that is required for social change serves to reinforce the prevailing status quo. As Micah White (2010) put it, 'clicktivism is to activism as McDonalds is to a slow-cooked meal. It may look like food, but the life-giving nutrients are long gone.' This point was made in a recent online advertising campaign by UNICEF in Sweden which carried the slogan 'likes don't save lives'. In one video a young boy says directly to the camera, 'sometimes I worry that I will get sick, like my mum got sick. But I think everything will be alright. Today, UNICEF Sweden has 177,000 likes on Facebook.'

In a related critique, Andrew Darnton and Martin Kirk (2011: 29) draw on Malcolm Gladwell's (2010) work to suggest that by keeping the 'barriers to entry' low, by asking supporters to commit only minimal time or money to the cause, barriers to leaving a relationship with an NGO will also be low. The result is a shallow and fleeting engagement with issues that helps to alleviate any residual feelings of guilt or responsibility for not having taken action. By way of evidence for this argument, Darnton and Kirk (2011: 29) suggest that examples of effective online organizing all have in common a move from initial online engagement to subsequent offline actions. This is precisely what One Billion Rising, Kony 2012 and the IF campaign all aimed to achieve.

In summary, while new technologies may allow for an increased range of actions, the key question is whether they are more likely to provoke a sustained commitment to action or fuel 'a race to the bottom of political engagement' (White 2010).

Power asymmetries in the technologies of viewing Finally, the very nature of traditional media technologies used by NGO campaigns, such as television and printed material, has been accused of reflecting and consolidating the unequal power relations between the global North and South (Chouliaraki 2006: 4). 'Old' media technologies allow for the 'safe' to watch the 'suffering', but not vice versa. This power imbalance is also evident in the audiences' ability to turn away from encounters with distant suffering when they choose, in contrast to suffering others themselves who cannot escape the reality of suffering so easily. As Jean Baudrillard (1994) suggests, 'the mediated face makes no demand on us, because we have the power to switch it off, and to withdraw'. Finally, the properties of the television screen itself have been held responsible for 'anesthetizing' (Chouliaraki 2006: 25) audiences from the moral demands of distant suffering. As Zygmunt Bauman (1993: 177) put it, 'there is, comfortingly, a glass screen to which their lives are confined ... They become flattened out, a property only of the screen, a surface, denied any moral compulsion because they are disembodied and disindividulated ... something other than human'.

In this context, new media technologies may appear to have the capacity to overcome the distance between audiences and suffering others and to challenge entrenched hierarchies of human life in ways which traditional technologies do not. In particular, new media technologies can allow distant others to speak for themselves and even converse directly and in real time with audiences through web chats, forums and social media. They also provide users with the opportunity to immerse themselves in other (virtual) worlds. The Save the Children Kroo Bay website, for example, includes a series of 'webisodes', which allow users to travel through various virtual scenes documenting elements of life in Kroo Bay, a village in Sierra Leone. Users can explore the town and the projects that have been set up as they wish and watch short films produced by local people. Users can also send online messages to Kroo Bay residents, who can themselves contribute to the conversation (Smith 2011).

Despite such opportunities, though, the potential 'anesthetizing' role of the medium persists. In particular, there is a danger that in remediating, or combining, 'old' forms of media, new media technologies contribute to the fictionalization of distant suffering. As Russell Watkins (2010) explains, 'the nature of the online interactive does borrow a certain visual language from the world of the video game, as well as from that of soap-opera and drama'. Kennedy (2009) adds that, in certain cases, online media simply provide new ways to 'fetishize suffering or exoticize the other', rather than eliciting genuine concern for a cause. He refers to 'virtual field trips' offered by CARE and quotes site user comments; 'within minutes, we are zooming through the outskirts of Guatemala City, "oohing" and "ahhing" over the lush terrain surrounding us'. In this case, new technologies can render audiences ineffectual 'virtual tourists' (ibid.) rather than engaged and active global citizens.

Moreover, internet users have a tendency to stick to what they are familiar and comfortable with. As a result, users without pre-existing interests in development are unlikely to search for, or stumble across, development content online. By contrast, chance encounters with distant others are much more likely on television, where serendipity plays a much greater role in determining consumption habits (Fenyoe 2010). Finally, while new media may allow for seemingly direct communication to take place between those in the North and those in the South, this does not automatically negate all power differentials. The digital divide ensures that such conversations will still likely be mediated, either by local elites who have greater access and control over local technologies, or by NGOs, which can regulate the format and even the content of such exchanges (Benthall 2010). The wider point is that while new technologies may provide alternative, and probably more complex, combinations of mediation as immediacy and hypermediacy, encounters with distant suffering online remain mediated encounters. As such, the medium will always interfere in some way in the process of overcoming distance between audiences and distant others.

The key tensions in humanitarian communication It should be apparent from the above discussion that the tensions associated with NGO campaigns are more deeply rooted than techno-logy alone (Smith 2011). Regarding hierarchies of human life, the very real economic and political divisions which exist in the world stem, not from technologies of communication, but from differences in economic resources, political stability, govern-mental regimes and, ultimately, unequal relationships of power (Chouliaraki 2006: 4). While technologies may reflect and even reinforce discourses of global inequality, they do not produce them. Moreover, it is difficult not to reflect such hierarchies of human life when the justification for NGOs work relies upon them.

Regarding the complexities of development, the need for fund-raising means that it is not in the interests of most NGOs to reveal the full realities of suffering, and of their imperfect efforts to alleviate it. Regarding action, a sustained commitment to effective action vis-à-vis distant suffering is contingent upon far more than the strategies or technologies used by NGO cam-paigns. How audiences respond to the various promises NGO campaigns make about the efficacy of the actions they suggest depends upon individual personalities and personal circum-stances. More broadly, the range of options for action audiences have open to them and the actual effects of those actions depend upon much larger political, economic and institutional realities.

In summary, new technologies do appear to have the capacity to ameliorate some of the key tensions associated with NGO campaigns by providing more context and greater opportun-ities for action, and challenging power asymmetries. However, certain tensions are deeply rooted in economic differences and political and geographical realities which cannot be redressed with technology. Ultimately, new technologies may be a useful tool, but it is the constraints faced by those using them which will determine the nature of their use (Smith 2011).

Conclusion

The central argument in this chapter is that there is no ideal strategy of humanitarian communication. All forms of humanitarian communication, through whatever medium, are subject to the same inherent tensions, to which there are no clear solutions. The tendency to simplify communications, for example, will remain as long as NGO communications have to compete for the fleeting attention of a largely cynical public in order to raise money.

In this context, I have suggested that it is useful to conceive of different forms of humanitarian communication, not as better or worse examples of representations, but as attempts to overcome distance in communication through alternative combinations of immediacy and hypermediacy. Whereas shock effects and deliberate positivism favour immediacy over hypermediacy, post-humanitarian communication preferences hypermediacy. New technologies may appear to offer more sophisticated forms of mediation, but ultimately the presence of the medium will always interfere with the process of overcoming distance between audiences and distant others.

The purpose of making this argument is not to criticize NGOs for their communication practices, whatever strategies they choose. Readers should not come away with the feeling that all forms of humanitarian communication are equally problematic. Instead, I hope this chapter has made it easier to appreciate more fully the choices and inevitable compromises involved in NGO communication so that we can assess and enter into these practices with our eyes wide open. More generally, I have shown that any account of the role of media in development must recognize the fact that the media are not an independent force acting upon society but are shaped by their relations with other processes in society.

6 | Media Coverage of the Global South: Who Cares?

With the introduction of the subject of media representations of development in the previous chapter, the focus of attention in this book shifted from South to North and from the *capacity* of organizations and individuals to take part in communication (media development) to the *substance* of communications. In this chapter, the discussion moves even farther away from the conventional territory of development studies and much more firmly into the traditional concerns of media studies. The aim of this chapter is to consider how media representations of the global South in general, and not just representations of development, might matter for development itself.

This agenda entails a further shift in focus; away from the communication practices of conventional development actors, such as NGOs, towards a much wider range of media actors, such as the news media and even entertainment media. This expanded focus derives partly from the fact that NGOs get their messages out, not just through their own communications, but increasingly through their interactions with the media (Cottle and Nolan 2007). But more than this, it stems from a recognition that one of the key consequences of globalization is that the activities of organizations in one part of the world are increasingly bound up with people's lives in other, distant, parts of the world.

To be clear, this chapter does not aim to repeat the now well-rehearsed claims regarding the apparent inadequacies of Western media coverage of the global South (see Fair 1992;

Brookes 1995; Hagos 2000; DfID 2000; Campbell 2007) or the various organizational and ideological explanations for this (see Shoemaker and Reese 1996; Schudson 1997; DfID 2000; Mezzana 2005). Instead, in line with the broader aim of this book, the intention here is to provide a rare critical review of a number of reasons why media representations, outside of those generated and circulated by conventional development actors, might also matter for development. Why might it matter, for example, if the number of international documentaries on UK television is in steep decline? Or if such programmes are found to cover the same topics, in the same formats, featuring the same parts of the world, every year, with very little variation (Scott 2011)? Specifically, this chapter will review the media's possible impact on overseas aid budgets, the formation of cosmopolitan sentiments and global relations of power. In doing so, it further stretches our understanding of development to include, not just formal development interventions by governments or NGOs, but the uneven encounter between the global North and South more generally. The conclusion of this chapter is that although there is reason to believe that media representations of the global South are intimately linked, in various ways, to international development, revealing how much they matter and in precisely what ways is especially challenging.

This difficulty in identifying a clear causal connection between media content and its effects is important because it shapes donors' willingness to support media coverage of development and the global South. In 2011, the UK Department for International Development (DfID) cut all of its funding for media activities directed at building support for development in the UK, based on the following conclusion of a report which it commissioned:

Raising awareness of development issues in the UK is likely

to contribute to reducing global poverty but it is not possible to establish a direct link or quantify the contribution made by DfID-funded activity. Therefore, a decision to continue funding activity in this area cannot be entirely evidence-based. (Dominy et al. 2011: 2)

So long as donors require there to be clear lines of causality between the work that they fund and the outcomes achieved, support for media representations of development will likely not be a priority.

The media's influence on foreign aid budgets

When asked, 'what is the most important issue facing Britain today?', fewer than ten out of 4,789 respondents cited any issue relating to global poverty (Hudson and Van Heerde-Hudson 2012: 3). '88% of EU citizens and 89% of citizens of the United States have not heard of the Millennium Development Goals' (Eurobarometer 2005; United Nations Foundation 2010).

The significance of statistics such as these derives, at least partly, from the assumption that how the public in donor countries thinks and feels about aid and development influences public policy about it. As is argued in a World Bank working paper on the subject, 'In recent years donor countries have committed to dramatic increases in the supply of foreign aid to developing countries. Meeting and sustaining such commitments will require sufficient support among donor country voters and taxpayers' (Paxton and Knack 2008: 1).

Furthermore, since few members of the public have personal experience of international development efforts or travel to aid recipient countries, the media presumably play a key role in determining the nature of public support for official development assistance (ODA). Indeed, survey data show that the UK public reports the most important sources of information on the lives of 'poor people in Africa' as being television (87 per cent), newspapers (59 per cent), radio (18 per cent) and the internet (11 per cent), with the most frequently cited non-media source of information being 'family and friends' (5 per cent) (TNS 2008). These results are widely supported by a range of other qualitative studies (DfID 2000; VSO 2001; Scott 2009; Fenyoe 2010).

It may be tempting to conclude from this that, through acting on public opinion, the media have a significant impact on government aid budgets. However, such a claim about the apparent connection between media representations and development policy is, as we shall see, highly problematic.

The media's influence on public support for ODA The first key assumption in this argument is that media content has a direct influence on public opinion. Such an assumption is evident in two kinds of claim. First, there are optimistic accounts which argue (or assume) that media content has a strong, positive influence on public dispositions towards the global South. These accounts usually understand the role of the media in political and civic terms – as a source of information. Media coverage of the global South, it is assumed, creates a more informed public who will be more inclined to support higher levels of government spending on aid. For example, after being informed about levels of poverty in India, 30 per cent of respondents to a UK survey changed their view on aid to India – from being unsupportive of current levels to being supportive (Lindstrom and Henson 2011).

In a pessimistic counter-view, it is argued that the media promote cynical and stereotypical ways of understanding the world, rather than acting as a source of information. Thus, media exposure has the opposite influence on public dispositions towards the global South and on corresponding levels of support for overseas aid. For example, from the results of a binary logistic regression of a survey of public attitudes towards development, Jennifer van Heerde-Hudson and David Hudson (2010: 9) find support for their hypothesis that 'on average, awareness of events in developing countries from TV news or newspaper readership is *negatively* related to concern or support'. They conclude that 'the largely negative, sensationalistic and truncated nature of media coverage of global poverty works to reduce individuals' feelings of efficacy in solving the issue' (ibid.: 12).

Both the pessimistic and optimistic accounts agree, albeit from different standpoints, that the media have a direct influence on public support for overseas aid. However, both accounts also suffer from a number of key weaknesses which disrupt their rather simplistic claims of media effects (in addition to offering contradictory claims). Primarily, both accounts fail to pay sufficient attention to the ability of the audience to contest, negotiate and reject media content, assuming instead that audiences all respond to media content in the same, predictable, way. How we feel about levels of overseas aid depends upon all manner of factors, such as perceptions of aid effectiveness and levels of poverty in other countries. Some of these perceptions may well have been informed by the media, but they will also have been simultaneously negotiated through audiences' existing knowledge and attitudes and through the context of consumption. Attitudes towards foreign aid are refined through individual personalities, values, beliefs and interests, resulting in complex, contingent, contested and highly personalized standpoints. Individual media use is also a deciding factor, since the content of different texts is likely to offer very different influences. Thus, while the media may well have a role to play in informing public attitudes towards overseas aid, the nature of this influence will differ greatly between individuals and between different media. Media effects are certainly not direct, universal or predicable. While 30 per cent of participants in the aforementioned study may have appeared to change their minds when informed about levels of poverty in India, we do not know why they (said they) changed their minds, whether this was a temporary change of heart, or perhaps more importantly, why the remaining 70 per cent did not change their minds.

Rather than suggesting that media content has a direct effect on what individuals think regarding levels of ODA, perhaps a more fruitful way of conceptualizing the role of the media is to examine their influence on how issues are framed. Shanto Iyengar's (1990) study of the influence of the framing of poverty on the way people think about poverty adopts just such an understanding. For Iyengar, the media do not have a direct influence on particular elements of public disposition, but they can shape the way in which public dispositions are structured. In order to investigate this, Iyengar compares the ways in which poverty in the USA is framed by the media with the ways in which the US public understands poverty. He shows that the way people think about poverty is 'dependent on how the issue is framed. When news media presentations frame poverty as a general outcome, responsibility for poverty is assigned to society-at-large; when news presentations frame poverty as a particular instance of a poor person, responsibility is assigned to the individual' (ibid.: 19).

Iyengar (ibid.: 20) uses survey data to show also that the frames engendered by the media have 'powerful effects on judgement and choice'. In this case, the understanding of causal responsibility engendered by particular news frames influences 'the degree to which Americans hold government responsible for assisting the poor … [and] the amount of governmental assistance respondents are willing to award to poor people' (ibid.: 35). In sum,

Iyengar shows how the media can structure public dispositions, by making particular ways of understanding the world available and others less so. The point is that while the media may not have a direct and predictable effect on public support for ODA, there are more measured ways of thinking about the complex and subtle influences that the media do have.

The influence of public support on government aid budgets If media representations are linked to government spending on aid, then the second major assumption must be that public opinion influences government policy in this area. In the context of current international commitments to increase aid, levels of public support for ODA have indeed taken on greater salience. The UK, for example, has currently committed itself to ring-fencing and even increasing its aid spending, despite its austerity measures. Such a commitment to ODA can be maintained, it is frequently argued, only with support from the public (Collier 2007: 183; TNS 2008: 182). As the DfID explained in its strategy paper *Building Public Support for Development* in 2007, 'without ... building public support for development across the UK ... the prospects of achieving the [MDG and ODA] targets will be significantly weakened' (Lader 2006: 2).

Some evidence of a positive relationship between public support and government expenditure on aid can be found by comparing donor countries. Nordic countries, which have particularly high levels of support for aid, for example, also have high levels of ODA as a percentage of GNP, while the opposite is true for countries with low levels of public support, such as Germany. Marc Stern (1998: xii) argues that such correlations exist because 'where public support is well articulated and well informed, it can make the political price sufficiently high to both protect and increase aid'.

Despite correlations suggesting a clear link between public

attitudes and public policy, the causal chain that connects the two is in fact extremely unclear. Identifying what the public's attitude towards ODA actually is is extremely difficult. In public opinion surveys, for example, various unreliable measures of public attitudes towards the global South are used as indicators of, or understood to be equivalent to, public support for ODA. Expressions of 'concern for poverty in developing countries', for example, are often taken to be equivalent to 'public support for ODA', when they are two rather different issues. Even measures of 'support for current or increased levels of development assistance' are heavily influenced by what Hudson and Van Heerde-Hudson (2012) describe as a 'social desirability response bias' or the thought 'who is going to say no to this?' As a result, it would be unwise 'to simplistically assume that there exists any single or stable public "opinion" on such complex matters' (Pidgeona et al. 2008: 70). Furthermore, support for ODA is generally regarded as remarkably weak (Hudson and Van Heerde-Hudson 2012), famously being characterized by Ian Smillie (1996) as 'a mile wide and an inch deep'. Political parties' policies on international development are not a key election issue.

The point here is that if public opinion is so shallow, shifting and difficult to capture, how can it possibly influence policy (Holsti 1992)? As one US government decision-maker puts it, 'I would argue that there is no single public opinion, so how does one respond to a huge community, a public community of stakeholders, I don't think you can' (Intermedia 2012). The only time that public opinion is likely to have some influence is with respect to levels of short-term, humanitarian, aid, when it is often at its clearest and strongest (see Otter 2003).

Gorm Olsen (2001) adds that because strong public support for helping the poor has an outlet in the form of emergency assistance and support for NGOs, this leaves decision-making on ODA as elite-centred and 'top-down'. Governments therefore have a relative freedom in this policy area to pursue their sense of moral obligation to do the right thing, even if this goes against public opinion. Thus, it is important to make a distinction between *mass* public opinion, which may influence ODA only in certain contexts, and *elite* opinion, which may be far more important in influencing decision-making.

Importantly, there *are* some examples where public opinion does appear to have directly influenced policy in this area. In France and the USA, for example, public opinion appears to have played an important role in bringing HIV/AIDS to the forefront of the government's development agenda, even resulting in increased public funds to tackle the issue in the USA (Intermedia 2012; see also Robinson 1999 for a discussion of the 'CNN effect'). Despite this, the conclusion of a survey of US, UK, French and German policy-makers in this area was that, in general, 'public opinion seems to have less impact on policymaking in this sector than might have been expected, and most government decision-makers perceive other factors, such as data-based evidence, as considerably more important for policymaking than public opinion' (Intermedia 2012: 3).

As was discussed earlier, public support for ODA is itself a composite of and determined by a range of public attitudes towards the global South, whose causal relationship with media representations is, at best, difficult to determine. Thus, we can conclude that while there may be some link between the media and levels of ODA, the nature of this link is varied, contingent, indirect and extremely difficult to isolate. Media representations may matter for development, but influencing support for ODA and levels of government aid is not the most compelling example of their significance. This case is also important for disrupting taken-for-granted assumptions about the direct effects of the media and for highlighting the complex nature of both audiences and political processes.

The media's influence on cosmopolitan attitudes

The possible impact of the media on government aid budgets is just one of the many potential consequences that media-informed public attitudes can have for development. Decisions to give money to overseas charities, join protests, sign petitions, buy fair-trade goods and travel to other countries are all, to a greater or lesser extent, informed in some way by media representations.

Unfortunately, analyses of this more diffuse role of the media in the public's engagement with development issues have generally suffered from a lack of a coherent framework, or even an informed vocabulary. *Viewing the World*, for example, is a comprehensive and influential report produced by the DfID in 2000, designed to 'examine the role of television in public understanding of international affairs'. Throughout the report, however, there is no clear or consistent conceptualization of what it is about the media's impact on public cognition that is under investigation. In the 550-word conclusion, for example, references to the ways in which the public are disposed towards the global South are variously defined as 'engagement', 'interest', 'understanding', 'perceptions', 'appetite' and being 'informed'.

Similarly, it is argued in *Viewing the World*, as elsewhere, that media coverage of the global South is 'negative' and should be more 'positive'. Western publics are seen to have 'negative' perceptions and ways need to be found of using the media to encourage them to be more 'positive'. Yet this 'negative'/'positive' dichotomy is highly problematic because it grossly oversimplifies the complex and nuanced ways in which the global South is represented and how these representations influence public attitudes and behaviours. The following quotation is an anonymous response to a survey question which asked, 'to what extent do you agree that news coverage of developing countries is dominated by "negative" stories?' It sums up well the problems associated with the terms. 'Defining stories as "positive" or "negative" is reductive and even childish …The idea that it's "negative" to cover, for example, the earthquake in Haiti is just daft. Stories are interesting or dull, surprising or obvious, not positive or negative. Also, positive for whom? Chinese investment in Africa is seen as positive by some and negative by others.'

In light of these inadequacies, attention has recently turned to the concept of cosmopolitanism as a means of referring to (mediated) public sentiment vis-à-vis faraway strangers. The term has traditionally been associated with a particular under-standing of political governance which entails a more inclusive relationship between nations and individuals within nations (perhaps even aimed at a world government) (Delanty 2006). More recently, however, the concept has been 're-activated' (Vertovec and Cohen 2002: 1) by a wide range of social and political theorists in what Ulrick Beck (2002: 17) describes as 'a revolution in the social sciences'. One way in which the term has been 're-activated' has been in references to a particular disposition associated with a conscious 'openness' to cultural differences, which entails, first of all, a willingness to engage with the other (Hannerz 1990: 239; Tomlinson 1999; Vertovec and Cohen 2002). As Tomlinson (1999: 185) puts it, being cosmopolitan, or a 'citizen of the world', means having 'a disposition which is not limited to the concerns of the immediate locality, but which recognises global belonging, involvement and responsibility'. It is this sense of openness to the world which better captures what it is about public attitudes that influences our willingness to engage in development-related activities, such as eco-tourism, ethical consumerism or supporting NGOs.

Mediated cosmopolitanism If this sense of openness to others and to the world is at the heart of public willingness to be involved in development, the question then becomes, 'how does the media foster such a cosmopolitan disposition?' A critical review of the work of Bronislaw Szerszynski and Mark Toogood (2003) and John Urry (2002) is helpful for beginning to answer this question. First, they argue that the media have the potential to foster cosmopolitanism because of 'how [they produce and circulate] images of places, brands, peoples and the globe itself, and narratives of various figures, heroes and organisations' (Urry 2002: 4). In doing this, they provide a pervasive and continuous visible access to other people's experiences and existences. Having such 'access to the world', Szerszynski and Toogood (2003) argue, has the potential to dissolve the distinction between 'our' experiences and 'theirs' and make us reflect upon and perhaps do something about the conditions of faraway strangers.

While this may be an appealing view of the role of the media, it does not provide an account of *how* the increasing diffusion of information and images might help to stimulate and deepen a sense of global responsibility (Thompson 1995: 264). In her discussion of this argument, Chouliaraki (2006: 28–9) accuses those who make such claims of turning to 'wishful thinking' to explain this apparent effect of the media. 'Audiences, we are told, must turn their sense of responsibility "into a form of moral-practical reflection" because this is "the best – the only option we have" ... The dream ... is asserted, but the questing of how we get there is essentially ignored.' Put another way, no account is given of why having visible access to other people's experiences and existences should *dissolve* the distinction between 'our' experiences and 'theirs' and not reinforce them.

Secondly, visible access to other people's experiences and existences may also offer a space in which individuals can understand themselves in relation to the world by reflecting on their own social roles and identities (Szerszynski and Toogood 2003: 225). As Chris Barker (1999: 7) argues, television is a 'major and proliferating resource for the construction of cultural identity'. This view of mediated cosmopolitanism is based less on 'wishful thinking' and, in Barker's account at least, draws on a well-grounded 'active audience' approach to media effects. However, this argument is still problematic because it does not attend to the idea that audiences may not make use of the resources the media provide to produce a cosmopolitan identity, but instead may use them to inform equally valid, though morally opposite, communitarian identities. In their empirical study of public talk about globalization, for example, Zlatko Skrbis and Ian Woodward (2007: 734) find that accompanying discourses relating to a positive orientation to faraway others 'was a counter discourse of fear, exclusion, global homogeneity, and suspicion of global others'.

Thirdly, the proliferation of global images may at least lead to a banal sense of cosmopolitanism, or a 'banal globalism' (Szerszynski and Toogood 2003), in the same way that a proliferation of national symbols, such as flying flags on public buildings and identifying with one's own sports-heroes, constitutes a sense of 'banal nationalism' (Billig 1995). As evidence to support this claim, Szerszynski, Toogood and Urry find thousands of examples of various forms of global images on television over a twenty-four-hour period, including images of the Earth, aerial images of generic global environments and images of iconic exemplars who demonstrate global responsibility – such as Nelson Mandela.

Once again, however, there is no guarantee that a proliferation of global images will necessarily contribute to a sense of openness. The word banal is interpreted by Szerszynski, Toogood and Urry as something affirmative but an equally valid interpretation of the concept of 'banal globalism' would be in a pejorative or critical sense, as a staged, superficial reality (Halsall 2006: 3). Jean Baudrillard (1994), for example, would clearly regard the staged nature of the reality presented by global images as something shallow and artificial rather than something affirmative. In short, it is not clear why the proliferation of global images should lead to cosmopolitanism, rather than any other feeling of being in the world.

Finally, television is unique in being able to offer audiences an experience of simultaneous participation in global events through the act of watching something at the same time as millions of dispersed others. Just as Benedict Anderson (1983) argued that television helps to create the nation as an 'imagined community' by addressing many people simultaneously, so television can help to create an imagined *global* community in the same way. However, in this account, the media orient audiences, not towards distant others, but towards fellow spectators. As Chouliaraki (2006: 27) puts it, 'in this argument, technological immediacy – the images that bring the sufferer close to our home – does not act as testimony of the sufferer's pain, but as a guarantee of the co-presence of spectators'. Consequently, this should not be considered an account of how the media produce a cosmopolitan disposition but an account of how television connects 'us' to people who are already like 'us' because they share our privileged position in front of, rather than behind, the screen.

In summary, for many accounts of the way in which the media encourage a cosmopolitan disposition, there is an opposing, but equally plausible, explanation of the way in which the media encourage alternative dispositions. Put another way, such claims frequently commit the 'cosmopolitan fallacy' (Beck 2002: 29) of assuming that media coverage of the global South necessarily leads to an expansion of horizons. They fail to recognize 'the existence of an opposing force to that of cosmopolitanism: an immunizing and interiorizing force which might cancel out and indeed reverse any such trend' (Halsall 2006: 1).

The complexities of mediated cosmopolitanism Importantly, this critique holds not only for such optimistic arguments, but also for more pessimistic argument – or claims that the media *undermine* a sense of cosmopolitanism. For example, Keith Tester (2001) argues that the media create the conditions of 'incommensurability' by continually presenting audiences with a number of circumstances, all of which invite them to take action, but which together make it impossible to rationally arbitrate between them. Tester (ibid.: 137) defines 'incommensurability', in this context, as the existence of a plurality of moral arguments, 'each of which is rational in terms of its initial premise but which is incompatible with the initial premise of an alternative argument', the consequence of which is an absence of any possible consensus over what ought to be done. Thus, audiences are left 'unable to make any decisive and consensually valid ethical judgements' (ibid.: 54).

While this may be a plausible argument about the role of the media in undermining cosmopolitan dispositions, it is itself undermined by the fact that there *are* circumstances in which audiences do achieve some form of moral involvement with appeals to act through the media. Otherwise we would not be able to account for the scale of public responses around the world to the 2005 Asian tsunami or the 2010 Haiti earthquake, for example, or other instances in which publics do act in response to distant suffering. In short, the media do not always block cosmopolitan sentiments, just as they do not always invite them.

From this discussion, we can identify two contradictory, 'either/or', understandings of how the media shape cosmopolitan dispositions. In optimistic accounts the media necessarily encourage cosmopolitan dispositions, whereas in pessimistic accounts the media always promote opposing, communitarian, responses (Chouliaraki 2006). The potential of the media to promote a cosmopolitan disposition is 'at once inevitable and impossible' (Robertson 2010: 149). These accounts are not only contradictory, they also fail to adequately explain how media texts produce one response rather than another. This tension between broadly optimistic and pessimistic accounts dominates debates more generally about the effects of media coverage of the global South on audiences. They appear in accounts of the role of the media in fostering support for ODA, as we have seen earlier, as well as in accounts of the role of the media in charitable donations (see Moeller 1999) and civic engagement (Shaw 1996).

In *The Spectatorship of Suffering* (2006), Chouliaraki offers a means of moving beyond these unhelpful, 'either/or', narratives to achieve a more reliable answer to the question 'how does the media foster a cosmopolitan disposition?' She argues that the potential of the media to make audiences feel for distant strangers should be considered neither de facto possible, nor a priori impossible, but contingent upon the peculiarities of individual texts. In other words, Chouliaraki suggests that we examine how these competing arguments are seemingly resolved in specific examples of media content. In order to achieve this, Chouliaraki develops an elaborate theoretical and methodological framework, which she describes as an 'analytics of mediation'. This involves analysing how the central contradictions between the competing optimistic and pessimistic narratives are played out in individual texts. These contradictions include the competing claims that the media: (1) simultaneously establish and undermine the immediacy of distant others, (2) create a sense of proximity and distance and (3) render the audience as both active and as impotent (ibid.: 37). By examining empirically how these three contradictions are played out in individual texts we can determine what 'moral horizons' (ibid.: 46) are made available to audiences in any given text.

While the analytics of mediation may indeed provide a

useful way forward, it has its own inevitable limitations and 'blind spots' (see Cottle 2009). There are also other compelling frameworks for examining the production of a mediated sense of cosmopolitanism (see Robertson 2010). The main reason for discussing it here is because it helps remind us both of the limitations of grand claims about the nature of media influence and of the need for abstract theoretical claims to be grounded in empirical research. But while such abstract theoretical claims about how media representations affect the way we feel about the world may have their limitations, seen together, they do at least illustrate the need to take seriously the role that an institution increasingly embedded in our everyday lives has on our sense of responsibility to others in the world. It may be difficult, if not impossible, to pin down precisely *how* the media make us feel about acting on behalf of distant others. But it would also be unreasonable to deny that the media have a very real significance in the choices we make regarding our public participation, or lack thereof, in international development.

The media's influence on global relations of power

A political economy perspective While the impact of media coverage on public attitudes might provide perhaps the most obvious link between media representations of the global South and development, it is not the most well cited nor, arguably, the most consequential. From a political economy perspective, such representations can be linked to all manner of phenomena – from influencing levels of international trade and investment, to legitimizing Western interventions in Iraq and Afghanistan.

In general terms, political economy approaches to media representations are concerned with how the ideological content of the media is controlled by those with power in order to maintain a system of values and beliefs that serve elite interest (Shoemaker and Reese 1996: 222). Thus, political economy approaches shift the focus of attention away from the apparent influence of media representations on individuals' attitudes and behaviours and towards the *function* of media representations within society more generally.

When it is applied specifically to the study of representations of the global South, those adopting this approach argue that such representations reflect and reinforce imbalances of power between different countries and between the global North and South in general. Put another way, representations of the global South are seen to matter, not for how they influence public support for ODA or broader public engagement with development, but for their impact on a country's position within human society, their international clout and their possibilities of development (Mezzana 2005). In this context, analyses of how the global South appears in the media aim to reveal the existence of old and new forms of colonialism, cultural, political and economical imperialism and the maintenance of Western hegemony (ibid.).

From this perspective, media texts are understood to achieve their ideological function through the circulation of discourses. Discourses refer to the way issues get represented, or the use of language to reflect and shape social order as well as shaping individuals' interaction with society (Jaworski and Coupland 1999: 3). Examples of dominant discourses about the continent of Africa, for example, include Africa as being a place of darkness, a place where Westerners search for their morality, a place ruled by irrational tribalism, a place of savagery and witchcraft and as dependent upon the West and a burden to it (Brookes 1995). Such discourses can relate to social identities, such as race, social relations, such as colonialism and dependency, and systems of knowledge, such as Orientalism and tribalism (Fairclough 1995: 55).

For Michel Foucault, discourses do not simply reflect the world but produce it by constructing knowledge and reinforcing certain ideologies over others (see Rose 2001: 136). As Norman Fairclough (2003: 9) puts it, discourses matter for the way they 'contribute to establishing, maintaining and changing social relations of power, domination and exploitation'. David Campbell (2007: 357) explains it more simply when he writes that 'the media acts as a form of knowledge which establishes the conditions of possibility for geopolitics'. For example, the suggestion that Arab countries 'can't handle democracy' has been cited as vital in legitimizing the continued sale of arms to repressive governments in the Middle East and North Africa, prior to the Arab Spring. Similarly, Simon Anholt (2010: 1) argues that

> Over the decades, with the best intentions in the world, the relentless depiction of Africa as one single, hopeless basket-case has harmed the long-term development prospects of the whole continent. After all, while many people would happily donate money to a basket-case, few will think it prudent to invest in a basket-case, buy products or services produced in a basket-case, go on holiday to a basket-case, or hire somebody born and raised in a basket-case.

Thus, in a political economy approach, it is through the circulation of discourses about the global South that media representations are understood to matter for global relations of power.

Orientalism and beyond Perhaps the most famous example of a political economy argument in this context comes from Edward Said's *Orientalism* (1978). The central tenet of this famous book is that there is a long tradition in France and Britain in particular (and later in the USA) of a style of thought based on a clear distinction between 'the Orient' (the Middle East) and 'the

Occident' (Europe), or between East and West. In Said's (ibid.: 1) terms, the Orient is constructed as one of Europe's deepest and most recurring images of the other. Such a distinction is reproduced in a variety of means; through art, literary texts, historical records and academic studies, in which the Orient is constructed as 'a place of romance, exotic beings, haunting memories and landscapes'. This distinction serves not only to define the Orient, or the other, but also to define Europe, or the West, as its contrasting image. By constructing the Orient as irrational, barbaric, opulent and chaotic, for example, the West becomes defined as rational, civilized, prudent and law-abiding.

For Said (ibid.: 3), Orientalism is not just a 'style of thought', but a Western mode of discourse 'for dominating, restructuring, and having authority over the Orient'. He argues that

> without examining Orientalism as a discourse one cannot possibly understand the enormously systematic discipline by which European culture was able to manage – and even produce – the Orient politically, sociologically, militarily, ideologically, scientifically, and imaginatively during the post-Enlightenment period ... In brief, because of Orientalism the Orient was (and is not) a free subject of thought or action.

The distinction between Orientals and Europeans was originally forged, Said argues, to justify colonial intervention: since Europeans defined themselves as superior it became their duty to intervene in the Orient. In this way, Said links representations directly to material realities. The character of this Orientalist discourse and its implications for Western interventions is well summarized in the following statements by Karl Marx.

> We must not forget that these idyllic village communities, inoffensive though they may appear, had always been the solid foundation of Oriental despotism, that they restrained the

human mind within the smallest possible compass, making it the unresisting tool of superstition, enslaving it beneath the traditional rules, depriving it of all grandeur and historical energies. (Marx 1853a)

England has to fulfil a double mission in India: one destructive, the other regenerating – the annihilation of the Asiatic society, and the laying of the material foundations of Western society in Asia. (Marx 1853b)

In more recent times there have continued to be examples of media representations appearing to reinforce a stereotypical construction of the Orient in ways that are linked to the exertion of Western power over the Middle East. Carol Stabile and Deepa Kumar (2005: 766), for example, argue that the central framework employed to justify the US-led war in Afghanistan 'constructed the West as the beacon of civilization with an obligation to tame the Islamic world and liberate its women'. Specifically, the level of attention the US media gave to women's liberation in Afghanistan 'served as one of the pillars on which elites sought to sell the war to the US public'.

Despite its popularity and appeal, *Orientalism* has been criticized on a number of grounds, including its selective use of evidence and its failure to provide details of the precise causal sequence by which discourse translates into power (Lewis 1993). Nevertheless, this work was instrumental in inspiring a whole new set of approaches to understanding colonialism and imperialism which draw attention to representations, rather than economics. Similar accounts of the powerful effects of Western discourses regarding the construction of the self and the other can be found in Samuel Huntington's (1996) influential thesis on *The Clash of Civilisations*, Jan Nederveen Pieterse's (1995) account of how Western popular culture serves as an instrument of African oppression, and in the pervasive construction of

'The West and the rest', as discussed by Stuart Hall (1992). By allowing for the classification of societies, such discourses of 'them' and 'us' enable evaluation and comparison – emphasizing European or Western uniqueness and non-Western inferiority.

Media discourses about the global South can be seen to matter, not only for sustaining global power relations between the North and the South in general, but for how they support more specific national interests or political ideologies. Asgede Hagos (2000), for example, argues that the US media's tendency to neglect the African continent in the 1970s and 1980s suited political and ideological requirements, such as undermining communism. Similarly, Jo Fair (1992) suggests that the amount of coverage afforded to different crises in Africa is a reflection of Western governments' intentions to intervene, or not, in these crises. More recently, in a discourse analysis of Western media coverage of China, Marc Stanton (2007: 26) argues that the media present 'stereotypical images of the unstoppable monolith of Chinese development, the destroyer of traditional industries in the west, a vast seething mass of humanity relentlessly expanding, intent on eventual world financial domination'. Such claims form part of a wider 'demonizing China' argument in which the Western media are accused of advancing a distorted vision of China, in order to combat the apparent threat of this rising superpower.

The operation of power through discourse should not be understood as entirely one-way or uncontested, however. In a hegemony approach, control of media discourse is conceptualized more as a 'tug of war' between competing interests (in which power determines the relative outcome) rather than as determined entirely by any singular elite interest (Gitlin 1980: 251). For example, Wendy Willems (2005: 103) argues that the Zimbabwean government has frequently drawn upon British media framing of events for its own ends – to define the situation in Zimbabwe as a struggle against imperialism. She suggests that this has 'provided an effective cover-up of the injustices committed by the Zimbabwean government against its own people'. Similarly, the 'demonizing China' argument may itself be seen as part of a wider discourse of Chinese victimhood, used to generate nationalist sentiment in China (and perhaps also to draw attention away from censorship of the Chinese media). In addition, new communication technologies have expanded the range of opportunities for counter-hegemonic voices to be heard and to confront dominant discourses. During the Kenyan presidential elections in 2013, for example, the *#someonetellCNN* hashtag was widely used on Twitter in Kenya to criticize some Western media coverage of the elections and present alternative narratives.

Putting a political economy perspective in perspective One of the key criticisms of political economy approaches is that they often fail to explain how elite power functions in reality to ensure that media content is consistent with elite interests. One of the most sophisticated and well-cited attempts to do just this is the propaganda model, developed by Herman and Chomsky in *Manufacturing Consent* (1988). The propaganda model identifies five filters which impact upon the editorial decision-making process and the selection of news and which are a product of corporate control of mass communication. They include: concentration of media ownership, advertising as primary income, dependency on sources provided by elites, 'flak' used to discipline the media, and particular ideologies as control mechanisms. These filters operate as a form of self-censorship by filtering out news that is incompatible with elite interests. The consequence for the news output produced as a result of these filters is that it 'serve[s] to mobilise support for the special interests that dominate the state and private activity' (ibid.: xi).

In order to provide empirical evidence to support their model,

Herman and Chomsky (ibid.: 40) analyse the unequal treatment afforded to comparable international news stories in the US media. They find, for example, that the murder of 'worthy' victims, such as Jerzy Popieluszko, a Polish priest, receives more coverage (seventy-eight articles in the *New York Times*), compared to the murder of 'unworthy' victims, such as seventy-two religious victims in Latin America (which received only eight articles). Similarly, from a study of the number of articles addressing the El Salvadorean election in 1984 in the *New York Times*, sixty-two were found to support the US government's agenda, while only twenty were found to be incompatible with it. Furthermore, by presenting the elections as 'voting in the midst of guerrilla violence', the US media helped portray the election as a step towards democracy in the face of intimidation by left-wing rebels – a narrative which very much suited the US government's anti-communist agenda at the time.

While Herman and Chomsky may provide an appealing and seemingly logical model of how elites control media representations, critiques of the propaganda model have been numerous and compelling. Herman and Chomsky have been accused of not adequately describing how these filters operate in actuality (and how they have changed over time) (Schudson 1997: 12), of overlooking the varying contexts that owners and advertisers operate in (Golding and Murdock 1991: 79) and of failing to recognize that the interests of elites are not always agreed or easily defined (Robinson 2001: 530).

These claims and criticisms of the propaganda model are useful for illustrating the value and limitations of a political economy perspective in general. Any approach which seeks to provide a wide-ranging account of the role of the media in global relations of power will always be likely to struggle to explain precisely how media content conforms to elite interests – and to provide evidence of clear lines of causality between media representations and the exercise of power. Nevertheless, in this weakness lies its strength, since its broad focus allows it to capture the broader and less tangible implications of media representations as part of a political and economic system. This perspective is also valuable in stressing the role of media, not simply as a source of knowledge or understanding, but as being involved in the circulation of taken-for-granted assumptions about the world. One of the key roles of the academic, or any media-literate audience member, is to expose or denaturalize such discourses and question the interests they appear to serve.

This political economy approach to media representations also has wider implications for the study of media and development. If we accept that discourses about development, about other countries and about our relationship with them are important for relations of power, then this dramatically opens up the range of texts, genres and forms of media that are relevant to development. It matters not just how NGOs or news bulletins represent the global South, but how other parts of the world appear, or not, in other – often far more popular – media contexts, such as in literature, feature films, documentaries, travel programmes or even reality-TV-style programmes (Lewis et al. 2013). Indeed, reality-TV programmes may actually offer far greater opportunity for the appearance of counter-hegemonic discourses than brief news bulletins because of their capacity to humanize distant others, thereby disrupting conventional hierarchies of human life (see Scott 2013).

Conclusion

We emerge from this review of three possible consequences of media representations of the global South, just as we should, with no clear answer to the question of precisely how important the media are for development in this area. Common sense may suggest that media representations influence public support for government spending on development and we may expect that public opinion has at least some role to play in determining government policy in this area. However, any claims about a causal relationship between the media and levels of government aid are, in reality, extremely problematic. While there may be a stronger case for the media having a direct role in informing public engagement with development more generally, it is still not clear precisely what that role actually is. Only recently has the concept of cosmopolitanism and the work of authors such as Robertson (2010) and Chouliaraki (2006) enabled us to make significant progress in this area. Finally, if we adopt a political economy perspective, then a whole range of real-world consequences can be seen to stem from media representations. Despite this, though, there remains a lack of detailed accounts of precisely how power influences representations and how such representations reinforce power.

Given these issues, what conclusion can we reach? There are insufficient grounds for concluding that media representations do *not* matter. Equally, though, we cannot conclude with any certainty that media representations are essential drivers of any one of the issues discussed above. Therefore, the only way we can conclude is by recognizing that media content, in a variety of different forms, generated from a range of different organizations, is, in a number of different ways, likely to matter for development but that it is not possible to determine precisely how or to what extent.

In 2013 the Norman Lear Center at the University of Southern California set up the Media Impact Project, with over US$3 million in funding from the Bill and Melinda Gates Foundation and the Knight Foundation. The aim of the project is to 'measure how media influences the ways people think and act, and contributes to broader societal changes' (Green and Patel 2013). Such efforts to measure the impact of media representations are crucial in an environment where donors require value for money and commercial media organizations have a tendency to avoid broadcasting content about the global South. However, this chapter has demonstrated that they do not have an easy task. Representatives from the Bill and Melinda Gates Foundation say they have been 'told countless times by colleagues how hard – and impossible – this may be' (ibid.). At least they were warned.

Conclusion

> Independent media play a critical role in building and sustaining democracies, societies and economies around the world. They provide citizens with the information necessary to make informed political and economic choices. Independent media give voice to women, youth and minorities, along with dissident political opinions. They also improve communities by providing citizens with important information on health, the environment and rural development, and help people prevent and respond to disasters. (Graves 2007: 4)

How should we make sense of such broad and optimistic claims about the role of media in development? Can the media really do all these things? Which media and under what circumstances?

The main aim of this book has been to provide a concise and critical review of the main theories and debates within the fields of communication for development (C4D), media development and media representations of development that will allow readers to begin to answer such questions and engage critically with claims like the one above. This quotation is referring primarily to different aspects of C4D and media development. Readers of this book should not only be able to recognize this but also understand the associated characteristics and criticisms of each approach and the extent to which the two are compatible. Readers should also be aware of some of the alternative ways in which media can be linked to development which this quotation does not allude to.

This critical review of the literature is also important for enabling us to reach informed judgements about the priority that should be given to the study and support of media in development. How seriously should we treat claims about the cost-effectiveness of M4D interventions, for example? What are the merits of different M4D hybrids? On what basis can we justify supporting media coverage of the global South? This review can also inform how media-related interventions are designed and evaluated. What do baseline versus endline data comparisons reveal (and mask) about the impacts of media campaigns? What exactly should we be seeking to measure in evaluations of media development initiatives? And for those interested in a career at the intersection between media and development, this book provides a map from which to begin plotting their own contribution.

Media and development: three fields or one?

Common themes Looking back over the previous six chapters, we can identify a number of advantages of examining the fields of C4D, media development and media representations of development alongside each other. First, it enables us to identify common themes and challenges across the three subject areas. One key question for them all being: what are the implications of new technologies? It was argued in Chapter 1 that new technologies have often been incorporated into the M4D approach without affecting the design of such projects. Indeed, the major criticism of contemporary ICT-related development projects is that they have not learnt lessons from the failures of previous M4D interventions. In Chapter 2, new technologies were shown to offer a number of opportunities both for promoting and inhibiting participatory communication. However, it was also suggested that it might be more productive to focus, not on what new technologies allow, but on what each individual context requires. In the context of media development, although ICTs have generally been incorporated into traditional models, it was argued in Chapter 3 that they should, at the very least, force us to ask difficult questions about how media development interventions are conducted in the future. Regarding media representations of development, it was explained in Chapter 5 that while new technologies may enable NGOs to at least ameliorate some of the key tensions associated with humanitarian communications, ultimately their impact depends upon the constraints faced by those using them.

This final point about new media offering new opportunities but at the same time functioning within the same sociocultural, economic and political systems as 'old' media is the one with the greatest resonance among all three fields. New technologies can help us to achieve things we could not before, such as organize mass protests almost instantaneously or disseminate images rapidly among networks of thousands. In some cases these new possibilities may be genuinely empowering or transformative – but only when circumstances allow. New technologies do not, by themselves, transform the overall sociocultural, economic and political circumstances in which development interventions and non-institutional, citizen-driven change take place.

Looking beyond the implications of new technologies, perhaps the most important issue shown to be common to each field is the irresolvable challenge of pinning down the precise impact of media on development. Donor demands for clear lines of causality supported by robust evidence stretch across all three subject areas. But whether in the context of demonstrating the link between media development and development outcomes (Chapter 4), understanding the implications of media coverage of the global South (Chapter 6) or providing evidence of the impact of media messages on development-related behaviours

(Chapter 1), this is a demand that can never be fully met. Instead, claims about media effects in all three fields are often based on rhetoric, anecdote or simplistic claims about causation based only on evidence of correlation. The quotation that opened this chapter is illustrative of the idealistic and imprecise ways in which media are often said to be linked to development. Indeed, Anita Gurumurthy and Parminder Jeet Singh (2009: 1) identify one of two main discourses in the field of ICT4D as being an 'innocent, techno-fascinated worldview of technologists who like to see ICTs as neutral and equally beneficial to all, avoiding discourses of power around ICT use'.

While these kinds of claims may go some way towards raising the profile of the media in development, they certainly do not get us any closer to understanding the complex and multiple roles that the media actually have. To pursue this goal, all three fields face the same challenge of moving away from direct effect theories of media influence, and towards adopting a range of more considered accounts. This book has demonstrated that there *are* more subtle theories and concepts that better reflect the complexities and contingencies of media's role in development. These may not always suit the requirements of donors, though. Emphasizing the intrinsic rather than the instrumental value of media development, for example, or explaining the subtleties of the process of mediated cosmopolitanism, may not be entirely conducive to a successful funding application. Nevertheless, the underlying argument of this book is that, ultimately, it is better to be transparent about the difficulties of isolating media effects and to strive to generate more sophisticated accounts which engage with these difficulties head-on, rather than to pretend that the lines of causality are clear and testable.

In striving for a more considered understanding of the role of media in development, all three fields also need to become less media-centric and accept that while the media may be increasingly important in many different aspects of development, they remain only one aspect of the broad, complex processes which shape the world. It is not a contradiction to say that the media are both increasingly important for development yet still operate within clear constraints.

Broader terrains A closer integration of the fields of C4D, media development and media representations of development also helps to challenge our understandings of what development is. In particular, examining the implications of Western media coverage for development provides a rare opportunity to challenge the common assumption that the subject of international development exists only in the global South. Put more formally, it contributes to a post-colonial development agenda by stretching the boundaries of development practice and development scholarship beyond a focus on the other (Smith 2012: 12). It forces us to ask whether, as Tim Unwin (2006: 105) puts it, 'The problems facing developing countries have more to do with the policies and practices of people living in the richer countries of the world than they do with the conditions prevailing in the developing world itself.'

As argued in Chapters 1 and 3, this is precisely the kind of question that needs to be asked more often in the context of C4D and media development – but also in international development more generally.

The breadth of material covered in this book also dramatically opens up the range of actors whose activities we might consider relevant to development. Rather than focusing on the actions of donors, Chapters 2 and 3 emphasize the importance of community participation and indigenous efforts respectively. One of the key implications of the discussion of media representations in Chapter 6 was that the content of news media and even entertainment media can have very real (if difficult to isolate) consequences for the lives of people in other countries. In Chapter 1 the growing role of philanthropic foundations in development was discussed – and the ability of telecommunications companies to provide populations with communication networks surely makes them important actors as well. Thus, a broad consideration of the role of media in development in general helps stretch conventional understanding of who is involved in development activities and where development takes place.

This broader perspective on development is increasingly important because recent political mobilizations around the world have clearly demonstrated that the processes which sustain or challenge poverty and inequality are certainly not limited to the activities of the development industry in the global South. In reflecting on this issue, Oscar Hemer and Thomas Tufte (2012: 5–6) write that

> The challenge for us, at this moment, is to take a step back and reflect, to analyze and understand, rather than to impose development strategies. While ComDev historically has been about developing prescriptive recipes of communication *for* some development, it is high time we refocus our attention to the deliberative, non-institutional citizen-driven change processes, full of media uses and communicative practices, but emerging from a citizens' profound and often desperate reaction to this global Now ... While the crucial role of media and communication in processes of social change and development at last becomes evident, it is paradoxically not associated with the field of communication for development.

In this context, Hemer and Tufte are right to suggest that it may be more useful to speak of media's role in social change, rather than development. This term signals a broader understanding of development; associated with the pursuit of more loosely defined public goods involving a wider range of actors, including social movements and collective action. At the same time, it is significant that their focus is on the implications for the field of C4D. The final section of this conclusion makes clear that we will need to continue bridging, expanding and transcending the boundaries of existing fields of study if we hope to keep up with the media's ever changing role in development.

Joint ventures The broad range of discussions within this book also enables us to identify a number of concepts and ideas being used in one field that might also have real value in others. While Chapter 6 demonstrated that a political economy perspective is at the heart of studies of media representation of development, Manyozo (2012) argues that it is frequently missing from the study of C4D and media development. Indeed, only 2.2 per cent of the articles Christine Ogan and her colleagues (2009) find in their meta-analysis of academic literature on development communication are political economy analyses. This is important because it was this perspective which alerted us to the problematic assumptions inherent in the dominant good governance strand of media development in Chapters 3 and 4, and which drew attention to the potential role of the M4D approach in supporting corporate interests in Chapter 1. In the future, it is this perspective which will be most effective in challenging the dominant view of ICT4D as an opportunity to 'deploy ICTs in order to universalise market fundamentalism in all facets of life' (Gurumurthy and Singh 2009: 1). Thus, if there was only one thing we could gain from a closer integration of the three fields, it should be greater recognition of the value of a political economy perspective.

Another potentially valuable feature of the study of representations of development is the concepts of mediation, immediacy and hypermediacy. In media studies the term mediation is generally used to refer to 'the act of transmitting something through the media', or, more substantively, 'the overall effect of media institutions existing in contemporary societies, the overall difference that media make by being there in our social world' (Couldry 2008: 379). In Chapter 5 a more specific interpretation of this term was shown to be useful in allowing us to better understand the role of media in enacting audiences' encounters with distant suffering, rather than just making them possible. The concept of mediation, which is popular in media studies but is rarely applied in the context of international development, could also be useful to the study of C4D or media development. With regard to media development it may allow us to be more precise about the non-linear and two-way effects of the existence of media institutions as such, rather than just the effects of their outputs (Silverstone 2002b). With regard to participatory communication, Nick Couldry (2008: 389) argues that the term provides a flexible means of thinking about 'the complexity of the multiple, often dialectical processes through which the range of practices that we gather under the term "digital storytelling" will transform society and politics'.

Similarly, in Chapter 5 the concepts of immediacy and hypermediacy helped to separate out the different dimensions of mediation. They also demonstrated that no technology, no matter how advanced, can ever act independently of the social, cultural, political and economic circumstances in which it is situated. The same principle, or indeed concepts, may be equally useful in advancing our understanding of the role of new media in participatory communication for development – specifically, by drawing attention to the constructed nature of all communication and the axes around which this construction takes place. Moreover, these concepts help us to recognize that the properties of new technologies are not entirely unique; they do not represent a radical departure from the practices

202 MEDIA AND DEVELOPMENT

of previous technologies so much as a 're-mediation' them. Re-mediation refers to the representation of one medium in another (Bolter and Grusin 2000: 45), or, as Marshall McLuhan (1964: 1) once remarked, the thought that 'the "content" of any medium is always another medium'. This process of refashioning or repurposing the properties of other media is as central to 'old' media as it is to 'new' media. Indeed, in *Remediation: Understanding new media* (2000: 45–6), Bolter and Grusin argue that although 'the digital medium can be more aggressive in its remediation ... remediation is a defining characteristic of the new digital media'.

There are also a number of lessons from the fields of media development and C4D that can help to inform the study of media representations of development. The discussion of participatory communication in Chapter 2 revealed how new media can promote interactivity, debate, decentralized networks and greater individual autonomy. Yet these particular affordances of new technologies were noticeably absent from the discussion of new media's role in humanitarian communication in Chapter 5. If strategies of humanitarian communication aspire to contribute directly to community empowerment, rather than just raise money for NGOs, then there is much that can be learnt from the work of authors like Manuel Castells (1996) and Clay Shirky (2009).

These suggestions represent just some of the ways in which the study of media and development can benefit from a cross-pollination of ideas between different fields. Looking beyond the theories and ideas discussed explicitly in this book, there are also many other concepts in both development studies (such as resilience) and media studies (such as cultivation theory) which can be productively applied across (and even beyond) the three fields discussed here. One such concept, mentioned briefly in the Introduction but otherwise overlooked, is 'mediatization'. This term, which has gained significant traction in media studies in recent years, refers to the distinctive and consistent transformation of society brought about by a 'media logic' (Couldry 2008: 376). More specifically, mediatization describes how many different processes, objects and fields are now constrained to take on forms or formats suitable for media representation and/or how they depend upon media exposure (ibid.: 379). Illustrations of the transformative effects of a media logic have been well documented in the area of politics. Examples include changes in the character of debates in the UK's House of Commons when proceedings began being televised (Franks and Vandermark 1995), more general practices of 'packaging politics' in ways that will promote political parties and their policies to the public (Franklin 2004), as well as the suggestion that publics are increasingly responding to politics as an aesthetic phenomenon, rather than as a deliberative process (Meyer 2003).

This same media logic is having very real consequences for development as well. In a rare consideration of this issue, Ben Jones (forthcoming) argues that mediatization has caused NGOs working in development to become more like media organizations, to hold themselves accountable in new ways and to value their media and campaign desks more highly. More broadly, though, there are still many questions about the implications of the mediatization of development that remain unclear. How have understandings of what counts as development work been affected? To what extent are the policies and practices of development actors now shaped by a requirement to be defensible in the media (Meyer 2003)? Are the requirements of a media logic felt more or less acutely in humanitarian interventions as opposed to longer-term development projects, or in some countries and contexts more than others? How is mediatization transforming, not just development actors, but the broader processes which sustain poverty and inequality around the world?

To what extent is the process of mediatization implicated in modernization or new forms of dependency and/or imperialism?

Addressing such questions is crucial if we hope to understand the more pervasive effects of society's saturation by the media. It should also be clear that in discussing the process of mediatization and its consequences we have moved firmly out of the conventional terrain of the three fields with which this book has been concerned. The idea that development is becoming mediatized marks a clear departure from traditional concerns for the role of media in delivering information, facilitating participation, promoting good governance and democracy, raising money and circulating discourses of global inequality. This is important because it makes clear the fact that these three fields represent only a starting point for developing a broad, critical appreciation of the role of media in development.

References

Agamben, G. (1998) *Homo Sacer: Sovereign power and bare life*, Stanford, CA: Stanford University Press.

Alcorn, J., A. Chen, E. Gardner and H. Matsumoto (2011) 'Mapping donor decision making on media development', Media Map Project, Internews, World Bank Institute.

Allen, K. and I. Gagliardone (2011) 'Kenya case study snapshot of donor support to ICTs and media', Media Map Project, Internews, World Bank Institute.

Allen, T. and N. Stremlau (2005) 'Media policy, peace and state reconstruction', in O. Hermer and T. Tufte (eds), *Media and Glocal Change*, Gothenburg: NORDICOM, pp. 215–32.

Alvares, C. (1992) 'Science', in W. Sachs (ed.), *Development Dictionary*, London: Zed Books, pp. 219–32.

Anderson, B. (1983) *Imagined Communities: Reflections on the origin and spread of nationalism*, New York: Verso.

Anholt, S. (2010) 'Aid: the double-edged blade', www.simonanholt. com/Publications/publications-other-articles.aspx, accessed 15 June 2012.

Armah, S. and L. Amoah (2010)

'Media freedom and political stability in sub-Saharan Africa: a panel data study', *Journal of Economic Development, Management, IT, Finance and Marketing*, 2(2): 41–67.

Arnstein, S. (1969) 'A ladder of citizen participation', *Journal of the American Planning Association*, 35(4): 216–24.

Arora, P. and N. Rangaswamy (2013) 'Digital leisure for development: reframing new media practice in the global South', *Media, Culture & Society*, 35(7): 898–905.

Arsenault, A. and S. Powers (2010) 'Review of literature', Media Map Project, Internews, World Bank Institute.

ASI (Adam Smith International) (2013a) 'Communication and public awareness', www.adam smithinternational.com/content/ communication-and-public-awareness, accessed 1 March 2013.

— (2013b) 'Communication and public awareness', Advertisement feature, *Guardian*, www.guardian. co.uk/global-development-professionals-network/adam-smith-international-partner-zone/ effective-development-requires-effective-communication?CMP= twt_gu, accessed 1 March 2013.

Asiedu, C. (2012) 'Information communication technologies for gender and development in Africa', *International Communication Gazette*, 74(3): 240–57.

Bailey, O., B. Cammaerts and N. Carpentier (2007) *Understanding Alternative Media*, London: Open University Press.

Banda, F. (2009) 'Exploring media education as civic praxis in Africa', in D. Frau-Meigs and J. Torrent (eds), *Mapping Media Education Policies in the World*, UNESCO, pp. 225–43.

Banda, F. and G. Berger (2009) 'Assessing your media landscape: available instruments, their role and their limitations', in E. Peters (ed.), *How to Assess Your Media Landscape: A toolkit approach*, GFMD.

Bandyopadhyay, S. (2009) 'Knowledge-based economic development: mass media and the weightless economy', LSE Department of Economics Discussion Paper Series 74, pp. 338–65.

Baran, P. (1957) *The Political Economy of Growth*, New York: Monthly Review Press.

Barker, C. (1999) *Television, Globalization and Cultural Identities*, London: Open University Press.

Basorie, W. D. (2011) 'Indonesia freedom of information laws, one year on', *Jakarta Post*, www.thejakartapost.com/news/2011/04/28/indone-freedom-information-lawsia%E2%80%99s-one-year.html, accessed 15 January 2013.

Batabyal, S. (2012) *Making News in India: Star News and Star Ananda*, London: Routledge.

Baudrillard, J. (1994) *Simulacra and Simulation*, Michigan: University of Michigan Press.

Bauman, Z. (1993) *Postmodern Ethics*, Oxford: Blackwell.

Beck, U. (2002) 'The cosmopolitan society and its enemies', *Theory, Culture & Society*, 19(1/2): 17–44.

Becker, L., T. Vlad and N. Nusser (2007) 'An evaluation of press freedom indicators', *International Communication Gazette*, 69(1): 5–28.

Beltran, L. R. (1976) 'Alien premises, objects and methods in Latin American communication research', in *Communication and Development: Critical Perspectives*, Beverly Hills, CA: Sage, pp. 15–42.

Benthall, J. (2010) *Disasters, Relief and the Media*, Wantage: Sean Kingston Publishing.

Berger, G. (2010) 'Problematizing "media development" as a bandwagon gets rolling', *International Communication Gazette*, 72(7): 547–65.

— (2011) *Media in Africa 20 Years On: Our past, present and future*, Media Institute of Southern Africa.

Besley, T. and R. Burgess (2002) 'The political economy of government responsiveness: theory and evidence from India', *Quarterly Journal of Economics*, 117(4): 1415–51.

Bhagwati, J. (1995) 'Democracy and development: new thinking on an old question', *Indian Economic Review*, 30(1): 1–18.

Billig, M. (1995) *Banal Nationalism*, London: Sage.

Boal, A. (1979) *Theatre of the Oppressed*, London: Pluto Press.

Bohler-Muller, N. and C. van der Merwe (2011) 'The potential of social media to influence socio-political change on the African continent', Policy Brief no. 46 for the Africa Institute of South Africa.

Boltanski, L. (1999) *Distant Suffering: Morality, media and politics*, Cambridge: Cambridge University Press.

Bolter, J. and R. Grusin (2000) *Remediation: Understanding new media*, New York: MIT Press.

Bordenave, D. (1994) 'Participative communication as a part of building the participative society', in S. White (ed.), *Participatory Communication: Working for change and development*, London: Sage.

Boyd-Barrett, O. (1977) 'Media imperialism: towards an international framework for the analysis of media systems', in J. Curran, M. Gurevitch and J. Woolacott (eds), *Mass Communication and Society*, London: Edward Arnold, pp. 116–35.

Brookes, H. J. (1995) '"Suit, tie and a touch of juju" – the ideological construction of Africa: a critical discourse analysis of news on Africa in the British press', *Discourse & Society*, 6(4): 461–94.

Burgess, J. (2010) *Evaluating the Evaluators: Media freedom indexes and what they measure*, CIMA.

Cameron, J. and A. Haanstra (2008) 'Development made sexy: how it happened and what it means', *Third World Quarterly*, 29(8): 1475–89.

Campbell, D. (2007) 'Geopolitics and visuality: sighting the Darfur conflict', *Political Geography*, 26(4): 357–82.

Campbell, S. (2004) 'Defining information literacy in the 21st century', World Library and Information Congress, paper presented at the 70th IFLA General Conference and Council, August.

Carpentier, N., R. Lie and J. Serveas (2008) 'Making community media work', in J. Servaes (ed.), *Communication for Development and Social Change*, London: Sage, pp. 347–74.

Castells, M. (1996) *The Rise of the Network Society*, 1st edn, Chichester: Wiley-Blackwell.

— (2007) 'Communication, power and counter-power in the network society', *International Journal of Communication*, 1: 238–66.

— (2009) *Communication Power*, Oxford: Oxford University Press.

— (2010) *The Rise of the Network Society*, 2nd edn, Chichester: Wiley-Blackwell.

Chakravartty, P. (2009) 'Modernization redux? Cultural studies and development communication', *Television & New Media*, 10(1): 37–9.

Chalk, S. (2012) *Kony 2012: Succcess or failure?* London: I.B.Tauris.

Chongkittavorn, K. (2002) 'The media and access to information in Thailand', in R. Islam (ed.), *The Right to Tell: The role of mass media in economic development*, Washington, DC: World Bank, pp. 255–67.

Chouliaraki, L. (2006) *The Spectator-ship of Suffering*, London: Sage.

— (2010) 'Post-humanitarianism: humanitarian communication beyond a politics of pity', *International Journal of Cultural Studies*, 13(2): 107–26.

— (2011) '"Improper distance": towards a critical account of solidarity as irony', *International Journal of Cultural Studies*, 14(4): 363–81.

— (2013) *The Ironic Spectator: Solidarity in the age of post-humanitarianism*, Cambridge: Polity.

CIMA (2013a) 'Media development vs. media for development', cima.ned.org/media-development/media-development-vs-media-for-development, accessed 1 January 2013.

— (2013b) 'What is media develop-ment?', cima.ned.org/media-development, accessed 1 June 2012.

Cohen, S. (2001) *States of Denial: Knowing about atrocities and suffering*, Cambridge: Blackwell.

Colle, R. (2007) *Advocacy and Interventions: Readings in communication and development*, New York: Internet-First Univer-sity Press.

Collier, P. (2007) *Bottom Billion*, Oxford: Oxford University Press.

— (2008) 'Independent media as a critical driver of development – checks, balances, and building an informed citizenry', Paper presented at the Salzburg Global Seminar, 5 October.

Colm, A. (2013) 'How to … avoid pitfalls in participatory development', *Guardian*, www.guardian.co.uk/global-development-professionals-network/2013/apr/04/how-to-design-participatory-projects, accessed 4 April 2013.

CONCORD (2006) 'Code of conduct on images and messages', General Assembly of European NGOs.

Cooke, B. and U. Kothari (eds) (2001) *Participation: The new tyranny?*, London: Zed Books.

Coronel, S. (2010) 'Corruption and the watchdog role of the news media', in P. Norris (ed.), *Public Sentinel: News media and govern-ance reform*, Washington, DC: World Bank, pp. 111–37.

Cottle, S. (2009) *Global Crisis Re-porting*, London: Open University Press.

Cottle, S. and D. Nolan (2007) 'Global humanitarianism and the changing aid-media field', *Jour-nalism Studies*, 8(6): 862–78.

Couldry, N. (2008) 'Mediatiza-tion or mediation? Alternative understandings of the emergent space of digital storytelling', *New Media Society*, 10(3): 373–91.

Coyne, C. and P. Leeson (2008) 'Media as a mechanism of institutional change and reinforce-ment', Paper presented at the Association of Private Enterprise Education Meetings, Las Vegas, NV, 6–8 April.

— (2009) *Media, Development, and Institutional Change: New thinking in political economy*, Cheltenham: Edward Elgar.

Cramer, S. and M. Babak (2013) 'Despite good numbers, growth of Afghan media a story of pitfalls',

www.theglobalobservatory.
org/analysis/450-despite-good-
numbers-growth-of-afghan-media-
a-story-of-pitfalls.html, accessed
1 January 2013.

Curran, J. (2000) 'Mass media and
democracy: a reappraisal', in
J. Curran and M. Gurevitch (eds),
Mass Media and Society, London:
Edward Arnold.

Darnton, A. and M. Kirk (2011)
*Finding Frames: New ways to
engage the UK public in global
poverty*, BOND.

Dean, J. (2008) 'Media development
or media for development?:
wrong question – but what's
the right one?', Blog entry on
the Communication Initiative
Network, posted 19 September,
www.comminit.com/?q=global/
node/277011, accessed 15 June
2012.

Delanty, G. (2006) 'The cosmopolitan
imagination: critical cosmopolitanism and social theory', *British
Journal of Sociology*, 57(1):
25–47.

DfID (2000) 'Viewing the world:
a study of British television
coverage of developing countries',
Glasgow Media Group and 3WE
for DfID, July.

— (2006) 'Making governance work
for the poor', DfID White Paper,
13 July.

Djankov, S., R. La Porta, F. Lopez-
de-Silanes and A. Shleifer (2002)
'The regulation of entry',
Quarterly Journal of Economics,
117(1): 1–37.

DMI (2013a) 'Changing behaviours.
Saving lives', Development Media
International website, www.
developmentmedia.net/, accessed
15 January 2013.

— (2013b) 'Mass media: the evidence
base', Development Media International briefing, London.

— (2013c) 'Can mass media reduce
child mortality?', Development
Media International briefing,
London.

— (2013d) 'How mass media can
save a million lives', Development
Media International briefing,
London.

Dogra, N. (2007) 'Reading NGOs
visually: implications of visual
images for NGO management',
*Journal of International Develop-
ment*, 19(2): 161–71.

— (2012) *Representations of Global
Poverty: Aid, development and
international NGOs*, London:
I. B. Tauris.

Dominy, G., R. Goel, S. Larkins and
H. Pring (2011) 'Review of using
aid funds in the UK to promote
awareness of global poverty',
DfID.

Donohue, G., P. Tichenor and
C. Olien (2006) 'A guard dog perspective on the role of the media',
Journal of Communication,
45(2): 115–28.

Dunn, H. and S. Johnson-Brown
(2008) 'Information literacies
and digital empowerment in the
Global South', in UNESCO,
*Media, Communication, Informa-
tion: Celebrating 50 years of
theories and practice*, IAMCR,
pp. 78–103.

Edwards M. (1999) *Future Positive*,
London: Earthscan.

Ejboel, J. (2006) 'Press independence
needs a healthy bottom line', in

B. James (ed.), *Media, Development and Poverty Eradication*, Paris: UNESCO, pp. 65–6.

Escobar, P. (1999) 'Discourse and power in development: Michel Foucault and the relevance of his work to the Third World', in T. Jacobson and J. Serveas (eds), *Theoretical Approaches to Participatory Communication*, Cresskill, NJ: Hampton Press, pp. 309–35.

Eurobarometer (2005) 'Attitudes towards development aid', Special Eurobarometer 222, European Commission.

Fair, J. E. (1992) 'Are we really the world? Coverage of U.S. food aid in Africa, 1980–1989', in B. G. Hawk (ed.), *Africa's Media Image*, New York: Praeger, pp. 109–20.

Fairclough, N. (1995) *Critical Discourse Analysis*, Boston, MD: Addison Wesley.

— (2003) *Analysing Discourse: Textual analysis for social research*, London: Routledge.

Feek, W. (2008) 'A Rose by Any Other Name is Still a … the basis for one coherent Communication and Media Development field of work', www.comminit.com/node/271848, accessed January 2013.

Fenton, N. and V. Barassi (2011) 'Alternative media and social networking sites: the politics of individuation and political participation', *Communication Review*, 14(3): 179–96.

Fenyoe, A. (2010) 'The world online: how UK citizens use the internet to find out about the wider world', DfID.

Franklin, B. (2004) *Packaging Politics: Political communications in Brit-*ain's *media democracy*, 2nd edn, London: Bloomsbury Academic.

Franks, S. (2014) *Reporting Disasters: Famine, aid, politics and the media*, London: Hurst.

Franks, S. and A. Vandermark (1995) 'Televising parliament: five years on', *Parliamentary Affairs*, 48(1): 57–71.

Freedom House (2013) 'Freedom of the press 2013: Middle East volatility amid global decline', www.freedomhouse.org/report/freedom-press/freedom-press-2013, updated 1 May, accessed 1 May 2013.

Freire, P. (1970) *Pedagogy of the Oppressed*, London: Penguin Books.

Frère, M. (2011) 'The Democratic Republic of the Congo: case study on donor support to independent media, 1990–2010', Media Map Project, Internews, World Bank Institute.

GFMD (2005) 'Mission of the GFMD: the 19 points of the Amman conference 2005', gfmd.info/index.php/about_gfmd/gfmd_ mission_the_19_points_of_the_2005_amman_ conference/, accessed 1 December 2012.

Gibson, T. (2010) 'The limits of media advocacy', *Communication, Culture & Critique*, 3(1): 44–65.

Girardet, E. (1996) 'Reporting humanitarianism', in R. Rotberg and T. Weiss (eds), *From Massacres to Genocide: The media, public policy, and humanitarian crises*, Washington, DC: Brookings Institution.

Gitlin, T. (1980) *The Whole World is Watching: Mass media in the making and unmaking of the new left*, Berkeley: University of California.

Gladwell, M. (2010) 'Small change: why the revolution will not be tweeted', *New Yorker*, 4 October.

Glahn, B. (2009) 'Arguments for media development: a survey of literature and references', Special report for the Salzburg Global Seminar 2009.

Glennie, A., W. Straw and L. Wild (2012) 'UK public attitudes to aid and development: understanding public attitudes to aid and development', ODI/IPPR.

Golding, P. and G. Murdock (1991) 'Culture, communications and political economy', in J. Curran and M. Gurevitch (eds), *Mass Media and Society*, London: Edward Arnold, pp. 15–32.

Graves, P. (2007) 'Independent media's vital role in development', CIMA/NED.

Green, D. and M. Patel (2013) 'Gates and Knight Foundations fund new project to improve measuring media impact', Impatient Optimists blog, www.impatient optimists.org/Posts/2013/04/ Gates-and-Knight-Foundations-Fund-New-Project-to-Improve-Measuring-Media-Impact, accessed on 1 January 2013.

Gumucio-Dagron, A. (2001) *Making Waves: Stories of participatory communication for social change*, Rockefeller Foundation.

— (2003) 'Take five: a handful of essentials for ICTs in development', in B. Girard (ed.), *The One to Watch: Radio, new ICTs and interactivity*, Rome: FAO, pp. 21–39.

— (2008) 'Vertical minds versus horizontal cultures', in J. Servaes (ed.), *Communication for Development and Social Change*, London: Sage, pp. 68–85.

Gurumurthy, A. and P. Singh (2009) 'ICTD – is it a new species of development?', IT for Change Perspective Paper, www.itfor change.net/sites/default/files/ITfC/ ICTD_Species_ of_Devlp_Ed.pdf, accessed 15 March 2013.

Haas, E. (2005) 'Activist media, civil society and social movements', in W. de Jong, M. Shaw and N. Stammers (eds), *Global Activism, Global Media*, London: Palgrave Macmillan.

Habermas, J. (1989) *The Structural Transformation of the Public Sphere*, Cambridge, MA: MIT Press.

Hagos, A. (2000) *Hardened Images: The Western media and the marginalization of Africa*, Trenton, NJ: Africa World Press.

Hall, S. (1992) 'The West and the rest: discourse and power', in S. Hall and B. Gieben (eds), *Formations of Modernity*, Cambridge: Polity, pp. 275–332.

Halsall, R. (2006) 'Towards a phenomenological critique of "mediated cosmopolitanism"', Paper presented at the annual meeting of the ICA, Dresden International Congress Centre, Dresden.

Hannerz, U. (1990) 'Cosmopolitans and locals in world culture', in M. Featherstone (ed.), *Global Culture: Nationalism, globalization and modernity*, London: Sage, pp. 237–51.

Hartmann, P., B. Patil and A. Dighe

(1989) *The Mass Media and Village Life: An Indian study*, New Delhi: Sage.

Harvey, M. (ed.) (2007) 'Media matters: perspectives on advancing governance and development', Global Forum for Media Development, Internews.

Haskell, T. (1985) 'Capitalism and the origins of the humanitarian sensibility', Part I, *American Historical Review*, 90(2): 339–62.

Hemer, O. and T. Tufte (2012) 'ComDev in the mediatized world', *Nordicom Review*, 33: 229–38.

Herman, E. and N. Chomsky (1988) *Manufacturing Consent: The political economy of the mass media*, New York: Pantheon Books.

Hobbs, R. (1998) 'The seven great debates in the media literacy movement', *Journal of Communication*, 48(1): 9–29.

Höijer, B. (2004) 'The discourse of global compassion: the audience and media reporting of human suffering', *Media, Culture & Society*, 26(4): 513–31.

Holsti, O. (1992) 'Public opinion and foreign policy: challenges to the Almond-Lippmann consensus', *International Studies Quarterly*, 36(4): 439–66.

Holtz-Bacha, C. (2004) 'What is "good" press freedom? The difficulty of measuring freedom of the press worldwide', Paper prepared for presentation at the 2004 conference of the IAMCR, Porto Alegre, Brazil, 25–30 July.

Howard, P. and M. Hussain (2013) *Democracy's Fourth Wave?: Digital Media and the Arab Spring*, Oxford: Oxford University Press.

Hudson, D. and J. van Heerde-Hudson (2012) '"A mile wide and an inch deep": surveys of public attitudes towards development aid', *International Journal of Development Education and Global Learning*, 4(1): 5–23.

Huesca, R. (2002) 'Participatory approaches to communication for development', in B. Mody (ed.), *International and Development Communication*, London: Sage, pp. 209–27.

Hume, E. (2005) 'Freedom of the press', *Issues of Democracy*, December, usinfo.org/enus/media/pressfreedom/docs/freedomofpress.pdf, accessed 15 January 2013.

Huntington, S. (1996) *The Clash of Civilisations and the Remaking of World Order*, New York: Simon & Schuster.

Inagaki, N. (2007) 'Communicating the impact of communication for development: recent trends in empirical research', Working Paper Series, Development Communication Division, World Bank, Washington, DC.

Intermedia (2012) 'Government decision-makers' perceptions of the impact of public opinion on international development: findings from France, Germany, the U.K., and the U.S.', Intermedia.

Islam, R. (2002a) 'Into the looking glass: what the media tell and why: an overview', in R. Islam (ed.), *The Right to Tell: The role of mass media in economic development*, Washington, DC: World Bank, pp. 1–27.

— (ed.) (2002b) *The Right to Tell:*

The role of mass media in economic development, Washington, DC: World Bank.

ITU (2013) 'Key ICT indicators for developed and developing countries and the world', Geneva: International Telecommunications Union.

Iyengar, S. (1990) 'Framing responsibility for political issues: the case of poverty', *Political Behavior*, 12(1): 19–40.

Javuru, K. (2012) 'Media development and media freedom', Blog post, kennedyjavuru.wordpress.com/category/media-freedom/page/2/, accessed 15 January 2013.

Jaworski, A. and N. Coupland (1999) *The Discourse Reader*, London: Routledge.

Jenkins, R. and A. Goetz (1999) 'Accounts and accountability: theoretical implications of the right-to-information movement in India', *Third World Quarterly*, 20(3): 603–22.

Jones, B. (forthcoming) 'International NGOs and their use of media'.

Kalathil, S. (2003) 'Battling SARS: China's silence costs lives', *International Herald Tribune*, 3 April.

— (2008) 'Scaling a changing curve: traditional media development and the new media', CIMA.

Kaplan, D. (2012) 'Empowering independent media: U.S. efforts to foster a free press and an open internet around the world', CIMA/NED.

KARF (2008) *Kenya Audience Research: Establishment phase*, Kenya Advertisers Research Foundation.

Katz, E. and P. Lazarsfeld (1955) *Personal Influence: The part played by people in the flow of mass communication*, New York: Free Press.

Kaufman, D. (2012) 'On media development: an unorthodox empirical view', Presentation at event on media development, CIMA, Washington, DC, 30 January.

Keane, J. (1991) *The Media and Democracy*, Cambridge: Polity.

Kellner, D. and J. Share (2005) 'Toward critical media literacy: core concepts, debates, organizations, and policy', *Discourse: Studies in the Cultural Politics of Education*, 26(3): 369–86.

Kennedy, D. (2009) 'Selling the distant other: humanitarianism and imagery-ethical dilemmas of humanitarian action', *Journal of Humanitarian Assistance*, sites.tufts.edu/jha/archives/411, accessed 1 June 2012.

Kinnick, K., D. Krugman and G. Cameron (1996) 'Compassion fatigue: communication and burnout toward social problems', *Journalism and Mass Communication Quarterly*, 73(3): 687–707.

Knudsen, L. (2006) *Reproductive Rights in a Global Context*, Nashville, TN: Vanderbilt University Press.

Krug, P. and M. Price (2002) 'The legal environment for news media', in R. Islam (ed.), *The Right to Tell: The role of mass media in economic development*, Washington, DC: World Bank, pp. 187–207.

Lader, D. (2006) 'Public attitudes toward development: knowledge and attitudes concerning poverty in developing countries, 2005', Office for National Statistics.

Lamers, M. (2005) 'Representing poverty, impoverishing representation? A discursive analysis of an NGO's fundraising posters', *Graduate Journal of Social Science*, 2(1): 37–70.

Lawrence, E., H. Farrell and J. Sides (2009) 'Self-segregation or deliberation? Blog readership, participation and polarization in American politics', *Perspectives on Politics*, 8(1): 141–57.

Lennie, J. and J. Tacchi (2011) *United Nations Inter-agency Resource Pack on Research, Monitoring and Evaluation in Communication for Development*, New York: United Nations.

— (2013) *Evaluating Communication for Development: A framework for social change*, Abingdon: Routledge.

Lerner, D. (1958) *The Passing of Traditional Societies*, Glencoe: Free Press.

Lewis, B. (1993) *Islam and the West*, Oxford: Oxford University Press.

Lewis, D., D. Rodgers and M. Woolcock (eds) (2013) *Popular Representations of Development*, London: Routledge.

Lidchi, H. (1999) 'Finding the right image: British development NGOs and the regulation of imagery', in T. Skelton and T. Allen (eds), *Culture and Global Change*, London: Routledge.

Lindstrom, J. and S. Henson (2011) 'What does the public think, know and do about aid and development?', IDS.

Lines, K. (2009) *Governance and the Media: A survey of policy opinion*, London: BBC World Service Trust.

Lissner, J. (1977) *The Politics of altruism: A study of the political behaviour of voluntary development agencies*, Geneva: Lutheran World Foundation.

— (1981) 'Merchants of misery', *New Internationalist*, 100(23): 23–5.

Locke, J. (1689) *Two Treatises of Government*, New York: Filiquarian Publishing.

Locksley, G. (2008) 'The media and development: what's the story?', World Bank Working Paper 158, Washington, DC.

MacKinnon, R. (2012) *Consent of the Networked: The worldwide struggle for internet freedom*, New York: Basic Books.

Mansell, R. (1982) 'The "new dominant paradigm" in communication: transformation versus adaptation', *Canadian Journal of Communication*, 8(3): 42–60.

Manyozo, L. (2011) 'Rethinking communication for development policy: some considerations', in R. Mansell and M. Raboy (eds), *The Handbook of Global Media and Communication Policy*, Chichester: Wiley-Blackwell.

— (2012) *Media, Communication and Development: Three approaches*, London: Sage.

Manzo, K. (2008) 'Imaging humanitarianism: NGO identity and the iconography of childhood', *Antipode*, 40(4): 632–57.

Martin, R. (1994) 'The mass media:

image and reality. Review of "Africa's Media Image" by Beverly G. Hawk', *Journal of Modern African Studies*, 32(1): 183–9.

Marx, K. (1853a) 'The British rule in India', *New York Herald Tribune*, 25 June.

— (1853b) 'The future results of British rule in India', *New York Herald Tribune*, 8 August.

McCall, E. (2011) *Communication for Development: Strengthening the effectiveness of the United Nations*, New York: United Nations.

McCombs, M. and A. Reynolds (2002) 'News influence on our pictures of the world', in J. Bryant and D. Zillmann (eds), *Media Effects: Advances in theory and research*, London: Routledge, pp. 1–16.

McLuhan, M. (1964) *Understanding Media: The extensions of man*, New York: McGraw-Hill.

McMillan, J. and P. Zoido (2004) 'How to subvert democracy: Montesinos in Peru', *Journal of Economic Perspectives*, 18(4): 69–92.

Melkote, S. and L. Steeves (2001) *Communication for Development in the Third World: Theory and practice for empowerment*, London: Sage.

Merkel, K. (2012) Unpublished manuscript, University of East Anglia, Norwich.

Meyer, T. (2003) *Media Democracy*, Cambridge: Polity.

Mezzana, D. (2005) 'A cancerous image: the causes of Africa's negative and reductive image', *African Societies*.

Mill, J. S. (2003 [1859]) *On Liberty*, New Haven, CT: Yale University Press.

Milton, J. (1644) *Areopagitica: A speech of Mr John Milton for the Liberty of Unlicenc'd Printing, to the Parlament of England*.

Moeller, S. (1999) *Compassion Fatigue: How the media sell disease, famine, war, and death*, New York: Routledge.

— (2009) 'Media literacy: understanding the news', CIMA.

Morozov, E. (2011) *The Net Delusion: How not to liberate the world*, London: Penguin Books.

Morris, N. (2005) 'The diffusion and participatory models: a comparative analysis', in O. Hermer and T. Tufte (eds), *Media and Glocal Change*, Gothenburg: NORDICOM.

Mottaz, L. (2010) 'U.S. government funding for media development', CIMA.

Mouffe, C. (1999) 'Deliberative democracy or agonistic pluralism', *Social Research*, 66(3): 746–58.

Müller, T. (2013) 'The long shadow of Band Aid humanitarianism: revisiting the dynamics between famine and celebrity', *Third World Quarterly*, 34(3): 470–84.

Myers, M. (2012a) 'Support to media where media freedoms and rights are constrained: what works and why?', Global Synthesis Report, London: BBC Media Action.

— (2012b) 'Is there a link between media and good governance? What the academics say', CIMA.

Nelson, A. (2009) 'Experimentation

and evolution in private U.S. funding of media development', CIMA.

Nelson, M. and T. Susman-Peña (2012) 'Rethinking media development: report on the Media Map Project', Media Map Project, Internews, World Bank Institute.

New Internationalist (1981) 'The big four: the new information order', *New Internationalist*, 100.

Nixon, R. (1960) 'Factors related to freedom in national press systems', *Journalism Quarterly*, 37(1): 13–28.

Norris, P. (2008) 'The role of the free press in promoting democratization, good governance and human development', in M. Harvey (ed.), *Media Matters: Perspectives on advancing governance and development*, GFMD, pp. 66–76.

— (ed.) (2010) *Public Sentinel: News media and governance reform*, Washington, DC: World Bank.

Norris, P. and R. Inglehart (2010) 'Limits on press freedom and regime support', in P. Norris (ed.), *Public Sentinel: News media and governance reform*, Washington, DC: World Bank, pp. 193–215.

Norris, P. and S. Odugbemi (2010a) 'Assessing the extent to which the news media act as watchdogs, agenda setters and gatekeepers', in P. Norris (ed.), *Public Sentinel: News media and governance reform*, Washington, DC: World Bank, pp. 379–93.

— (2010b) 'Evaluating media performance', in P. Norris (ed.), *Public Sentinel: News media and governance reform*, Washington, DC: World Bank, pp. 3–31.

Norris, P. and D. Zinnbauer (2002) 'Giving voice to the voiceless: good governance, human development and mass communications', Occasional paper, Human Development Report Office, UNDP.

Nyamnjoh, F. (2005) *Africa's Media: Democracy and the politics of belonging*, New York: Zed Books.

Obregon, R. (2012) 'Social media and communication for development: towards an equity perspective', in R. Braskov (ed.), *Social Media and Development Cooperation*, Ørecomm Festival, Malmö University, pp. 64–80.

Ofcom (2006) 'Media literacy audit: report on media literacy amongst children', stakeholders.ofcom. org.uk/market-data-research/media-literacy/archive/medlitpub/medlitpubrss/children/, accessed 15 January 2011.

Ogan, C., M. Bashir, L. Camaj, Y. Luo, B. Gaddie, R. Pennington, S. Rana and M. Salih (2009) 'Development communication: the state of research in an era of ICTs and globalization', *International Communication Gazette*, 71(8): 655–70.

Olsen, G. (2001) 'European public opinion and aid to Africa: is there a link?', *Journal of Modern African Studies*, 39(4): 645–74.

Otter, M. (2003) 'Domestic public support for foreign aid: does it matter?', *Third World Quarterly*, 24(1): 115–25.

Panneerselvan, A. S. and L. Nair (2008) *Spheres of Influence*, Kathmandu: Panos South Asia.

Panos (2003) *Missing the Message?*

20 years of learning from HIV/ AIDS, London: Panos Institute.

Paxton, P. and S. Knack (2008) 'Individual and country-level factors affecting support for foreign aid', World Bank Policy Research Working Paper 4714.

People's Daily (2009) 'Chinese president urges global media to promote world peace, development', english.people.com.cn/ 90001/90776/90883/6778098.html, accessed 15 May 2012.

Pidgeona, N., I. Lorenzoni and W. Poortinga (2008) 'Climate change or nuclear power – no thanks!', *Global Environmental Change*, 18(1): 69–85.

Pieterse, J. N. (1995) *White on Black: Images of Africa and blacks in Western popular culture*, New Haven, CT: Yale University Press.

Plewes, B. and B. Stuart (2007) 'The pornography of poverty: a cautionary fundraising tale', in D. Bell and J. Coicaud (eds), *Ethics in Action*, Cambridge: Cambridge University Press, pp. 23–37.

PMC (Population Media Centre) (2013) *Acting for Change*, www.populationmedia.org/, accessed 20 January 2013.

Prochaska, J., C. DiClemente and J. Norcross (1992) 'In search of how people change: applications to addictive behaviours', *American Psychologist*, 47(9): 1102–14.

Putzel, J. (2010) 'The role of the media in fragile states: can donors help improve the quality of journalism?', ODI Event report, 8 October.

Putzel, J. and J. van der Zwan (2005) 'Why templates for media development don't work in crisis states', LSE Research online report.

Radley, A. and M. Kennedy (1997) 'Picturing need: images of overseas aid and interpretations of cultural difference', 3(4): 435–60.

Ram, N. (1995) 'An independent press and anti-hunger strategies', in J. Drèze, A. Sen and A. Hussain (eds), *The Political Economy of Hunger*, Oxford: Oxford University Press.

Reinikka, R. and J. Svensson (2004) 'The power of information: evidence from a newspaper campaign to reduce capture', Working Paper 3239, Washington, DC: World Bank.

Right2info (2012) 'Access to information laws: overview and statutory goals', right2info.org/access-to-information-laws, accessed 1 June 2012.

Robertson, A. (2010) *Mediated Cosmopolitanism: The world of television news*, Cambridge: Polity.

Robinson, P. (1999) 'The CNN effect: can the news media drive foreign policy?', *Review of International Studies*, 25(2): 301–9.

— (2001) 'Theorizing the influence of media on world politics: models of media influence on foreign policy', *European Journal of Communication*, 16(4): 523–44.

Rogaly, B. and B. Taylor (2009) *Moving Histories of Class and Community: Identity, place and belonging in contemporary England*, Basingstoke: Palgrave Macmillan.

Rogers, E. (1962) *Diffusion of Innovations*, New York: Free Press.

— (1969) *Modernisation among Peasants: The impact of communication*, New York: Rinehart & Winston.

Rose, G. (2001) *Visual Methodologies: An introduction to the interpretation of visual materials*, London: Sage.

Said, E. (1978) *Orientalism*, New York: Pantheon Books.

Sajo, A. (2003) 'From corruption to extortion: conceptualization of post-communist corruption', *Crime, Law and Social Change*, 40: 171–94.

Sankore, R. (2005) 'The pitfalls and consequences of development "pornography"', www.global envision.org/library/8/766, accessed 5 March 2010.

Schramm, W. (1964) *Mass Media and National Development: The role of information in the developing countries*, Paolo Alto, CA: Stanford University Press.

Schudson, M. (1992) *Watergate in American Memory: How we remember, forget and reconstruct the past*, New York: Basic Books.

— (1997) 'The sociology of news production', in D. Berkowitz (ed.), *The Social Meaning of News: A text reader*, London: Sage, pp. 7–22.

Scott, M. (2009) 'The world in focus: how UK audiences connect with the wider world and the international context of news in 2009', IBT/CBA.

— (2013) 'More news is bad news: expanding the scope of studies of "the public faces of development"

and "media and morality"', in D. Lewis, D. Rodgers and M. Woolcock (eds), *Popular Representations of Development: Insights from novels, films, television and social media*, London: Routledge.

Scott, M., Rodrigueaz-Rojas, S. M. and Jenner, C. (2011) 'Outside the box: how broadcasters portrayed the world in 2010', UKAID/IBT.

Sen, A. (1999) *Development as Freedom*, Oxford: Oxford University Press.

Servaes, J. (1989) *One World, Multiple Cultures: A new paradigm on communication for development*, Leuven/Amersfoort: Acco.

— (1990) 'Rethinking development communication: one world, multiple cultures', *Journal of Development Communication*, 1(2): 35–45.

— (1995) 'Development communication – for whom and for what?', *Communication*, 21(1): 39–45.

— (1996) 'Participatory communication and research in development settings', in J. Servaes, T. Jacobson and S. White (eds), *Participatory Communication for Social Change*, New Delhi: Sage, pp. 13–25.

Servaes, J. and P. Malikhao (2005) 'Participatory communication: the new paradigm?', in O. Hermer and T. Tufte (eds), *Media and Glocal Change*, Gothenburg: NORDICOM.

Shaffer, P. (2012) 'Post-development and poverty: an assessment', *Third World Quarterly*, 33(10): 1767–82.

Shaw, M. (1996) *Civil Society and*

Media in Global Crises: Representing distant violence, London: Pinter.

Shirky, C. (2009) *Here Comes Everybody: How change happens when people come together*, London: Penguin Books.

— (2011) 'The political power of social media', *Foreign Affairs*, 90(1): 28–41.

Shoemaker, P. and S. Reese (1996) *Mediating the Message: Theories of influences on media content*, London: Longman.

Silverstone, R. (2002a) 'Mediating catastrophe: September 11 and the crisis of the other', *Dossiers de l'Audiovisuel*, 105: 2–10.

— (2002b) 'Complicity and collusion in the mediation of everyday life', *New Literary History*, 33(5): 745–64.

— (2006) *Media and Morality: On the rise of the mediapolis*, Cambridge: Polity.

Siu-nam Lee, P. (1994) 'Mass communication and national development in China: media roles reconsidered', *Journal of Communication*, 44(3): 22–37.

Skrbis, Z. and I. Woodward (2007) 'The ambivalence of ordinary cosmopolitanism: investigating the limits of cosmopolitan openness', *Sociological Review*, 55(4): 730–47.

Slater, D. (2013) *New Media, Development and Globalization: Making Connections in the Global South*, Cambridge: Polity.

Smillie, I. (1996) 'Mixed messages: public opinion and development assistance in the 1990s', in C. Foy and H. Helmich (eds), *Public Support for International Development*, Paris: OECD, pp. 27–54.

Smith, M. (2012) 'Public imaginaries of development and complex subjectivities: the challenge for development studies', Paper prepared for the symposium 'Capitalism, Democracy, and Celebrity Advocacy', University of Manchester, 19/20 June.

Smith, M. and H. Yanacopulos (2004) 'The public faces of development: an introduction', *Journal of International Development*, 16(5): 657–64.

Smith, R. (2011) 'Development discourses online: a social semiotic analysis of the Save the Children Kroo Bay website', Unpublished Master's thesis, University of East Anglia.

Sobel, R., N. Dutta and S. Roy (2010) 'Beyond borders: is media freedom contagious?', *Kyklos*, 63(1): 133–43.

Sonderling, S. (1997) 'Development support communication: a change agent in support of popular participation or a double agent of deception?', *Communicatio*, 23(2): 34–42.

Sparks, C. (2007) *Globalization, Development and the Mass Media*, London: Sage.

Spivak, G. (1988) 'Can the subaltern speak?', in C. Nelson and L. Grossberg (eds), *Marxism and the Interpretation of Culture*, London: Macmillan, pp. 271–313.

Stabile, C. and D. Kumar (2005) 'Unveiling imperialism: media, gender and the war on Afghanistan', *Media, Culture & Society*, 27(5): 765–82.

Stanton, M. (2007) 'Gatekeepers: a critical discussion about the stereotypical presentation of the Chinese "other" by British TV news', *China Media Research*, 3(1): 26–32.

Stern, M. (1998) 'Development aid: what the public thinks', UNDP Development Studies Working Paper Series.

Stiglitz, J. (2002) 'Transparency in government', in R. Islam (ed.), *The Right to Tell*, Washington, DC: World Bank, pp. 27–45.

Straubhaar, J. (2000) *World Television: From global to local*, London: Sage.

Street, J. (2010) *Mass Media, Politics and Democracy*, Basingstoke: Palgrave.

Sunstein, C. (2008) 'Neither Hayek nor Habermas', 134(1/2): 87–95.

Susman-Peña, T. (2012) 'Healthy media, vibrant societies: how strengthening the media can boost development in sub-Saharan Africa', Media Map.

Szerszynski, B. and M. Toogood (2003) 'Global citizenship, the environment and the media', in B. Adam, S. Allan and C. Carter (eds), *Environmental Risks and the Media*, London: Routledge, pp. 218–28.

Tester, K. (2001) *Compassion, Morality and the Media*, London: Open University Press.

Tettey, W. (2010) 'Regional case studies of media roles: Saharan Africa', in P. Norris (ed.), Washington, DC: World Bank, pp. 277–305.

Thompson, A. (ed.) (2007) *The Media and the Rwanda Genocide*, London: Pluto Press.

Thompson, J. (1995) *The Media and Modernity: A social theory of the media*, Cambridge: Polity.

Thussu, D. (2007) 'The "Murdoch-ization" of news? The case of Star TV in India', *Media, Culture & Society*, 29(3): 593–611.

TNS (2008) *Public Attitudes towards Development*, London: DfID.

Tomlinson, J. (1999) *Globalization and Culture*, Cambridge: Polity.

Tufte, T. (2008) 'Fighting AIDS with edutainment: building on the Soul City experience in South Africa', in J. Servaes (ed.), *Communication for Development and Social Change*, London: Sage, pp. 327–47.

Tufte, T. and P. Mefalopulos (2009) 'Participatory communication: a practical guide', World Bank Working Paper no. 170, Washington, DC: World Bank.

Tufte, T. and N. Wildermuth (2013) 'African youth, media and civic engagement', in T. Tufte, N. Wildermuth, A. Hanson-Skovmoes and W. Mitullah (eds), *Speaking Up and Talking Back?*, Gothenburg: International Clearinghouse on Children, Youth and Media, pp. 11–19.

UNESCO (1991) *Declaration of Windhoek*, Seminar on Promoting an Independent and Pluralistic African Press, Windhoek, Namibia, 3 May.

— (2008) 'Media development indicators: a framework for assessing media development', International Programme for the Development of Communication.

United Nations Foundation (2010) 'Index of public opinion on international assistance and the Millennium Development Goals', Hart Research.

Unwin, T. (2006) 'Doing development research "at home"', in V. Desai and R. Potter (eds), *Doing Development Research*, London: Sage, pp. 104–12.

— (2013) 'The internet and development: a critical perspective', in W. Dutton (ed.), *The Oxford Handbook of Internet Studies*, Oxford: Oxford University Press.

Urry, J. (2002) 'The global media and cosmopolitanism', Paper presented at the Transnational America Conference, Bavarian American Academy, Munich, June.

Usdina, S., E. Scheepersa, S. Goldsteinb and G. Japhet (2005) 'Achieving social change on gender-based violence: a report on the impact evaluation of Soul City's fourth series', *Social Science & Medicine*, 61: 2434–45.

Van Heerde-Hudson, J. and D. Hudson (2010) '"The righteous considereth the cause of the poor"? Public attitudes towards poverty in developing countries', *Political Studies*, 58(3): 389–409.

Vertovec, S. and R. Cohen (2002) *Conceiving Cosmopolitanism: Theory, context and practice*, Oxford: Oxford University Press.

VSO (2001) *Live Aid Legacy: The developing world through British eyes*, London: Voluntary Services Overseas.

WACC (2005) 'The no-nonsense guide to communication rights', WACC.

Waisbord, S. (2000) *Family Tree of Theories, Methodologies and Strategies in Development Communication*, New York: Rockefeller Foundation.

— (2005) 'Five key ideas: coincidences and challenges in development communication', in O. Hermer and T. Tufte (eds), *Media and Glocal Change*, Gothenburg: NORDICOM.

Wallack, L. and L. Dorfman (1996) 'Media advocacy: a strategy for advancing policy and promoting health', *Health Education Quarterly*, 23(3): 293–317.

Watkins, R. (2010) 'From real people to virtual villages: Katine to Kroo Bay', *Developing Pictures: Photography+Development*, developingpictures.wordpress. com/2010/11/11/06-from-real-people-to-virtual-villages-katine-to-kroo-bay/, accessed 5 August 2011.

Weaver, D. (1977) 'The press and government restriction: a cross-national study over time', *International Communication Gazette*, 23(3): 152–70.

Weber, M. (1930) *The Protestant Ethic and the Spirit of Capitalism*, London: Unwin Hyman.

White, M. (2010) 'Clicktivism is ruining leftist activism', *Guardian*, guardian.co.uk/ commentisfree/2010/aug/12/ clicktivism-ruining-leftist-activism, accessed 5 August 2011.

White, S. (1994) *Participatory Communication: Working for change and development*, London: Sage.

Wilkins, K. and F. Enghel (2013) 'The privatization of development through global communication industries: living proof?', *Media, Culture & Society*, 35(2): 165–81.

Willems, W. (2005) 'Remnants of empire? British media reporting on Zimbabwe', *Westminster Papers in Communication and Culture*, Special issue, pp. 91–108

Wilson, M. and K. Warnock (2007) *At the Heart of Change: The role of communication in sustainable development*, London: Panos.

Wolfensohn, J. (1999) 'Voices of the poor', *Washington Post*, 10 November.

World Bank (1999) *Voices of the Poor*, Washington, DC: World Bank.

— (2001) *Consultations with the Poor*, Washington, DC: World Bank.

— (2002) 'The media', in World Bank, *The World Development Report 2002*, ch. 10, Washington, DC: World Bank.

Index

About Zed Books

Zed Books is a critical and dynamic publisher, committed to increasing awareness of important international issues and to promoting diversity, alternative voices and progressive social change. We publish on politics, development, gender, the environment and economics for a global audience of students, academics, activists and general readers. Run as a co-operative, Zed Books aims to operate in an ethical and environmentally sustainable way.

Find out more at:

www.zedbooks.co.uk

For up-to-date news, articles, reviews and events information visit:

http://zed-books.blogspot.com

To subscribe to the monthly Zed Books e-newsletter, send an email headed 'subscribe' to:

marketing@zedbooks.net

We can also be found on **Facebook**, **ZNet**, **Twitter** and **Library Thing**.